HIGH PERFORMANCE DJANGO

by Peter Baumgartner and Yann Malet

COPYRIGHT

ORDERING INFORMATION

Special discounts are available on quantity purchases by corporations, associations, and others. For details, contact us at:

http://lincolnloop.com/ ↗

ACKNOWLEDGEMENTS

Thanks to everyone at Lincoln Loop who chipped in to make this book possible, especially our designer, Mark Wirblich, and editor, Valerie Coulman.

A special thanks to the Kickstarter backers. Without their support, this book would never have been written.

Corporate Backers

- Divio https://www.divio.ch/ ↗
- Django Stars http://djangostars.com/ ↗
- Common Code https://commoncode.com.au/ ↗

Individual Backers

- Jonathan Chu
- Joe Bergantine
- Nick Albright
- Alex Gustafson
- Larry T. Brice
- Wouter Luberti
- Jannis Leidel
- Tianyi Wang
- Shige Abe
- Ernesto Rico-Schmidt
- paurullan
- Christian Assing
- Bjorn Pettersen
- Jason Mulligan
- Steve Jalim
- Todd Jefferson
- Michael Hale
- Marco Beri
- Sebastian Dieser
- Vidir Gudmundsson
- Henk Vos
- Griffin Caprio
- Stephen Wolff
- Derek Rodger

- Andrew Abbott
- Kyle Getrost
- Sid McLaughlin
- Zhu Yuzhou
- Josh Batchelor
- Anggriawan Sugianto
- Anthony Lupinetti
- Eugene Liang
- Tordbjørn Wang Eriksen
- Ibai
- Nicholas Fiorentini
- Marwan Alsabbagh
- Reto Aebersold
- Cícero Raupp Rolim
- Chris Curvey
- Frank Bieniek
- Wen Chun Lin
- Raphaël Hertzog
- Matthias Erll
- Michal Gonda
- Richard Davis
- james robb
- Stefan Jansen
- Patrick Toal
- Maurits Van Wijland
- Chris Erickson
- Paul Davis

- Michael MacKinnon
- Ryan Rathsam
- Ojas Amin
- Brendon John Muschamp
- Larry Meirosu
- Sébastien Fievet
- Loïc Espern
- Jim
- Mikael Andersson
- Ryan Palmer
- Trent
- Frederic Tschannen
- Gillingham
- Rune Thor Mårtensson
- Victor Allen
- Pesach Weinstock
- Manuel Miranda
- Arkadiusz Tułodziecki
- Peter Hanley
- Anatoliy Basov
- Roman Valls Guimera
- Rickard Steien
- Philippe O. Wagner
- Clint Shuman
- Dave Messina
- Alex M Spicer
- Diederick Hakkers

- Alan Si
- Adam Feuer
- Desmond Chen
- Senko Rašic
- Manuel Solórzano
- Rolo Mawlabaux
- Jose Padilla
- smartt
- Ryan Kaskel
- Tim White
- Drew Hubl
- Robert Cadena
- Karl Leuschen
- Yoshitaka Ishihara
- Börkur Guðjónsson
- Ashley Williams
- Eric Wallstedt
- Roberto Rosario
- Niclas Åhdén
- marteinn
- Tim Bell
- Nicole Turgeon
- Alex Church
- Frank Tobia
- Chip Standifer
- Micah Hausler
- Alec Perkins
- Paul McLanahan
- Ulrich Petri

CONTENTS

PREFACE

Thank you for picking up a copy of *High Performance Django*. When I started Lincoln Loop back in 2007, Django was still a pre-1.0 fringe player in the web framework world. It's come a long way since then and so has its supporting ecosystem. A lot of bad practices have shaken out and we now have a good blueprint for deploying stable, fast, and scalable Django sites.

The inspiration for this book came from a report I was writing for one of our clients. We were helping a company with a very large Django site (both in lines of code and daily visitors) troubleshoot and diagnose some mysterious scaling issues. Despite having a very bright and talented development team, they were missing quite a few quick and easy performance wins. Instead, much of the team's focus was around building and maintaining complex custom software to keep their site operational. It dawned on me that if an experienced team like this was struggling, what chance did your average developer have?

That night I started working on an outline, and over the next few months, we codified our techniques for building high performance Django sites into this book. After seven years of consulting, we've seen and built enough different Django sites to know what works and what doesn't. As you'll see, there are no hidden trade secrets. The tools we use are, for the most part, well known and in heavy use on many production Django sites. The thing is, though, there are a lot of pieces you need to put in place and one wrong decision can make life very difficult. You can follow all the conference talks and blog posts, but they only give you small windows into how it's done; nobody really puts together the full picture.

The goal of this book is to give you that blueprint so you can build and deploy high performance Django sites with confidence. We hope you enjoy it.

– Peter Baumgartner, co-author

THE BIG PICTURE

CHAPTER 1
THE BIG PICTURE

INTRODUCTION

It's not uncommon to hear people say "Django doesn't scale". Depending on how you look at it, the statement is either completely true or patently false. Django, on its own, doesn't scale. The same can be said of Ruby on Rails, Flask, PHP, or any other language used by a database-driven dynamic website. The good news, however, is that Django interacts beautifully with a suite of caching and load balancing tools that will allow it to scale to as much traffic as you can throw at it. Contrary to what you may have read online, it can do so without replacing core components often labeled as "too slow" such as the database ORM or the template layer.

Django's scaling success stories are almost too numerous to list at this point. It backs Disqus, Instagram, and Pinterest. Want some more proof? Instagram was able to sustain over 30 million users on Django with only 3 engineers (2 of which had no back-end development experience). Disqus serves over 8 *billion* page views per month. Those are some **huge** numbers. These teams have proven Django most certainly *does* scale.

Our experience here at Lincoln Loop backs it up. We've built big Django sites capable of spending the day on the Reddit homepage without breaking a sweat.

Every site has unique needs and different pain points requiring extra attention to operate at scale. You may be surprised, however, to learn that their general approaches to the problem all look very similar. Perhaps even more surprising is that many parts of this infrastructure aren't even unique to Django applications. The techniques we'll use are widely accepted across high traffic sites of many frameworks and languages.

Our point is this: Django scales, and the tactics described in this book will help you build sites capable of withstanding millions of page views per day and hundreds, if not thousands, of concurrent users. We have years of experience applying these tactics on heavily trafficked production sites. It works for us and we're confident it will work for you too.

PHILOSOPHY

❚❚ *Simplicity is a prerequisite for reliability.*
EDSGER W. DIJKSTRA

For our team at Lincoln Loop, the guiding philosophy in designing high-traffic Django sites is **simplicity**. Without making a conscious effort to fight complexity at every turn, it is too easy to waste time building complex, unmaintainable monstrosities that will bite you down the road.

Simplicity means:

1. Using as few moving parts as possible to make it all work. "Moving parts" may be servers, services or third-party software.

2. Choosing proven and dependable moving parts instead of the new hotness.

3. Using a proven and dependable architecture instead of blazing your own trail.

4. Deflecting traffic away from complex parts and toward fast, scalable, and simple parts.

Simple systems are easier to scale, easier to understand, and easier to develop. Of course, any non-trivial web application will bring its own unique set of complex problems to solve but by keeping the rest of the stack simple, you and your team can spend more time focusing on your product rather than on scaling and infrastructure.

THE PAIN POINTS

Django apps, and for that matter, most web applications share many common performance characteristics. Here are the most frequent pain points we encounter building performant web applications; they should look familiar to you.

DATABASE

A relational database (eg, Postgres, MySQL) is usually the slowest and most complex beast in the stack. One option is to replace it with a faster and less complex "NoSQL" database, but in many cases, that pushes the complexity into your application and squarely into the hands of your developers. We've found it simpler to keep it down in a proven RDBMS and handle the pain via caching.

TEMPLATES

Templates get complex quickly. To make matters worse, Django's template engine has made a trade-off for simplicity and usability over speed. We could replace it with a faster templating engine like Jinja2, but it will still be the second slowest part of our stack. We can avoid the pain via caching.

PYTHON

Python is "fast enough" for many workloads and the trade-off it provides by having mature developer tools and a mature ecosystem is well worth it.

The same can be said of just about every other mature dynamic scripting language. But we can serve requests faster from a web accelerator (e.g., Varnish) that can serve cached responses before a request even gets to the Python layer.

CACHE ALL THE THINGS

By now you probably see where we're headed. The simplest general approach is to cache all the way down the stack. No matter how fast and how well tuned your stack is, it will never be as fast as a dedicated cache.

Serving the entire HTTP response directly out of cache is ideal. When it isn't possible, as many parts of the response as possible should come from cache. Calls to the database can be kept to a bare minimum by implementing a caching layer there as well.

All this caching might sound like a nightmare for readers who know Phil Karlton's famous quote,

> ■■ *There are only two hard things in Computer Science: cache invalidation and naming things.*

In the following chapters, we'll teach you safe caching techniques to ensure your users never see stale content (unintentionally). Additionally, we'll show you how to tune your stack so it is as fast as possible, even on a cache miss.

Why the rush to cache?

Multi-layer caching lets us push the bulk of our traffic away from the more complex and custom built software onto battle-tested, high performance, open source software.

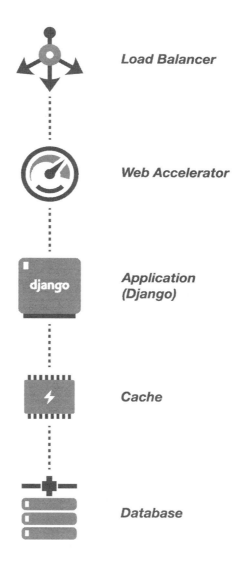

Load Balancer

Web Accelerator

Application
(Django)

Cache

Database

At each layer, load may be distributed horizontally across multiple systems. But the farther down the stack any given request travels, the slower and more taxing it will be on the infrastructure. Your goal, therefore, is to serve as much of your traffic from as high up the stack as possible.

The common players in this stack are:

- **Load Balancer:**

    - Open Source: HAProxy, Nginx, Varnish

    - Commercial: Amazon ELB (Elastic Load Balancer), Rackspace Clould Load Balancer

- **Web Accelerator:**

    - Open Source: Varnish, Nginx + Memcached

    - Commercial: Fastly, Cloudflare

- **App Server:** uWSGI, Gunicorn, Apache

- **Cache:** Memcached, Redis

- **Database:** Postgres, MySQL/MariaDB

THE JOURNEY OF A REQUEST

At first glance, all these different pieces of software can be daunting. In our consulting practice, we've seen sites that get the fundamentals of these functional elements wrong and end up with a fragile infrastructure held together with bailing wire and duct tape. It's critical to understand the purpose of each one and how they interact with each other before moving forward.

Let's use our imaginations and pretend you are a passenger in a magical vehicle that's taken the form of an HTTP request and is traversing the layers of the web stack. The journey starts in the browser where an unassuming user sends you on your way by typing the domain of your website in the address bar.

A DNS lookup will happen (unless you've set a high TTL (time to live) and the lookup is already cached). The lookup will point your vehicle to the IP address of your load balancer and send you rocketing off across the information superhighway to the different stops on your journey.

LOAD BALANCER

The first stop is your load balancer whose main responsibility is to dispatch traffic to your underlying infrastructure. It acts as a single proxy point that receives requests from the internet and dispatches them to healthy application servers (aka, the pool). It also does health checks and removes app servers from the pool if they are determined to be misbehaving.

Most load balancers let you choose an algorithm (e.g., round robin, least connections) for distributing requests to the application servers. It may also be possible to specify weights to force some servers to receive more traffic than others.

For most cases, round robin is a safe default. Routing traffic to the server with the least number of connections sounds like an amazing idea, but it can be problematic in some scenarios. Take, for example, adding application servers to the pool during a traffic spike. The new server will go from zero connections to a flood of connections as soon as it joins the pool. This can lead to an undesirable result: the new server is overwhelmed, declared unhealthy, and taken out of the rotation.

The load balancer is a good place to do SSL termination. This is the act of decrypting a request coming in via HTTPS and passing it down the stack as HTTP. It's good to do this early on in the stack. Speaking HTTP is easier and the load balancer usually has the spare CPU cycles to handle this task.

Depending on your choice of software, the load balancer may also have some overlapping functionality with the next layer on our journey, the web accelerator.

WEB ACCELERATOR

As your vehicle passed through the load balancer, it directed you to one of possibly many web accelerators at the next level of the stack. The web accelerator (aka, caching HTTP reverse proxy) is the first line of defense for your application servers farther down the stack. (In this book, we'll focus on Varnish[1], our preferred web accelerator solution.)

One of the first tasks for the web accelerator is to determine if this is a request for a resource where the response varies with each user. For many applications it might seem like *every* request varies per user. There are some tricks we'll show you later to work around this, but the basic question at the web accelerator is this: is this page unique to you or the same for everyone?

---

[1]   https://www.varnish-cache.org/

If the response is user-specific, it will wave your vehicle on to the next layer in the stack. If not, it will see if it already has a copy of the response in its internal cache. If it's found, your vehicle's journey stops here and you're sent back to the browser with the cached response. If it isn't found in cache, it will send you down the stack, but take a snapshot of the response on your way back so it can store it in the cache.

Ideally most requests' journeys end here. The web accelerator absorbs traffic spikes generated by a marketing campaign or viral content on sites like Reddit or Facebook.

Your journey is going to keep going, however. Next stop the application server!

APPLICATION SERVER

Up to now, you've been zooming along the high-speed interstate highway but as you start to pull into the application server, the road gets a little more winding and your pace starts to slow down.

The application server has a simple task, it turns your HTTP request into a WSGI (web server gateway interface) request that Python can understand. (Our preferred application server is uWSGI[2].) There are lots of lanes of cars passing through the application (aka WSGI) server and on the other side you catch sight of Django. The winding road now becomes city streets complete with turns and stop signs.

[2]   http://uwsgi-docs.readthedocs.org/en/latest/ ✎

DJANGO

The Django streets should look familiar to you. You go through the middleware, hand off your URL to the router who points you towards one of the views in the application. You notice, however, that there are a few differences between this Django application and the ones you hack on on your laptop.

Some requests are getting responses and zipping home in the middleware zone. That's Django's per-site cache in action. As you enter the view you notice that instead of having to stop and wait for every database query, some return out of cache almost immediately (a database query cache). Rather than twisting and turning through the template level, you notice some of the blocks simply fly by (template caching).

While slow compared to the highway you were on earlier, the trip through Django was pretty fast. You've now got the full response in tow and need to head home to the browser. On your way, you'll pass back through each layer, checking in a copy of your response with the per-site cache in Django and again with the web accelerator on your way out to the internet.

How long did your little request journey take? Surprisingly, all this happens in just a fraction of a second.

When you start looking at your own application's response times, here are some rough numbers you can shoot for. If your application is five times slower, there's going to be a lot of room for improvement.

Estimated Response Times	
10ms	Varnish cache hit
35ms	Django per-site cache hit
100-300ms	Django with warm cache
500ms-2s	Django with cold cache

Breaking it down further, for requests passing through to Django the total time spent should not be overwhelmingly dominated by a single component (database, cache, etc.). The majority of time should be spent working in Python with no more than 30% or so spent in any given component.

How's your Django app compare? Is there room for improvement? In the next chapter we'll explore the development process and show you how and where to optimize your application as you build it.

THE BUILD

CHAPTER 2
THE BUILD

▋▋ *Premature optimization is the root of all evil.*
DONALD KNUTH

Building a high-traffic site from scratch is a dangerous undertaking. There are lots of places Django can be optimized and it's easy to fall into a trap of optimizing things that won't need it. Trying to do it all grinds productivity to a halt and wastes months or even years of developer time. You need to separate the optimization you *need* from the time-wasting optimizations that won't make a difference.

Your biggest ally in this fight is real-world data. If you are replacing an existing site, looking at the existing data and traffic patterns over a long period is imperative. Knowing how existing users behave on the site will help you identify the hot spots requiring optimization. Saving a single database query on a page that sees a million hits a day is far more important than saving ten queries on a page that only gets one thousand views daily.

In many cases, you won't have any real-world data to work with but you can create your own. Pushing hard to soft-launch to a small group of users lets you collect performance data to see where optimization is required. Huge sites like Facebook and Etsy make heavy use of "feature-flippers" that allow them to turn on specific features to a subset of their users. This is discussed further in Launch Planning *(page 125)*.

Once you know where the hot spots are in your application, you can start optimizing by taking the easiest and least intrusive steps first (remember, our goal is simplicity). A good load testing environment will give you quick feedback on the effect of your changes and confidence when you've done enough optimization. This is discussed further in Load Testing with Jmeter *(page 108)*.

APPROACH

There are a few basic tenets to how we build Django sites that might not seem important now, but make a big difference down the road.

LOCAL DEVELOPMENT

A developer should be able to install and run the Django project wherever it is convenient for them: a laptop, virtual machine, docker container, or remote server. Too often we see teams throw their hands up in the air and say their application is too complex for this. In reality, that's rarely the case. Making the project easily installable will accelerate onboarding new developers and help fight back unnecessary complexity. The local development environment should be configured as closely as possible to production. If you use Postgres on your servers, don't use SQLite locally. Those subtle differences in your environments can be the source of ugly hard-to-track bugs.

SETTINGS ORGANIZATION

Some developers like to go crazy with their settings files, building complex file structures or introducing class-based inheritance schemes. Complexity is our sworn enemy. Instead, we try to maintain a simple setup, inspired by the 12 Factor[1] application philosophy.

At the root of our project, we create a `settings` module. Ideally this will just be a single file, but once a project gets sufficiently large that approach tends to be unrealistic. Rather than a one-size-fits-all file, we create a few sub-modules:

- `settings.base`

  The settings shared amongst all deploys. This should be the largest file of the bunch.

- `settings.dev`

  Common tweaks to get the project running locally, replacing any services that can't be run locally and enabling debugging.

---

[1]   http://12factor.net/ ↗

- `settings.deploy`

    A few tweaks for deployment such as implementing caching layers that would otherwise inhibit local development.

All settings inherit from `settings.base` so in `settings.deploy` you might see something like this:

```
from myproject.settings.base import *

TEMPLATE_LOADERS = (
    ('django.template.loaders.cached.Loader',
     TEMPLATE_LOADERS),
)
```

For sensitive information such as the `SECRET_KEY`, API keys, and external resources like the database location and credentials, we use our configuration management tool to inject them into the environment via environment variables. uWSGI can set environment variables using the `env` option[2]. In an `ini` formatted configuration file, that looks like this:

```
env = SECRET_KEY=abdefg12345hijklmno
env = DATABASE_URL=postgres://u:pw@dbhost:5432/name
```

This approach will get the variables into your web process, but the environment variables won't be available for running management commands. For these scenarios, you'll want to write them out to a `.env` file as well. You can load them into your environment for management

---

[2] http://uwsgi-docs.readthedocs.org/en/latest/Options.html#env ⬈

commands either by hacking `manage.py` with something like `dotenv`[3] or by using a simple Bash one-liner:

```
export $(cat .env | grep -v ^# | xargs)
```

Since the `.env` file is language agnostic, it is a great way to share settings between services written in different languages.

Accessing the environment variables in your settings is simple:

```
import os
SECRET_KEY = os.environ.get('SECRET_KEY')
```

One issue with environment variables is that they are always loaded in as a string. What about when you need a different object type like a boolean or a set? Don't worry, the built-in `ast` module has your back:

```
import ast
import os

DEBUG = ast.literal_eval(
    os.environ.get('DEBUG', 'True'))

# "/path/templates1,/path/templates2"
# converts to a tuple
TEMPLATE_DIRS = ast.literal_eval(
    os.environ.get('TEMPLATE_DIRS'))
```

One last helpful tip we use to prevent us from running with the wrong settings is to symlink it in each environment to `local.py`. Then we modify

---

[3] https://github.com/jacobian/django-dotenv ↗

`manage.py` to use this file by default. It cuts down on mistakes and saves the hassle of manually specifying the settings every time. You can find examples of these techniques in our Django template, `django-layout`[4].

BE CAUTIOUS OF THIRD-PARTY APPS

One strength of the Django ecosystem is the variety of high-quality reusable applications available on PyPI. Unfortunately, the vast majority of these applications were not written for high traffic scenarios. In many cases, they've traded off performance for ease of use and flexibility.

Building your site around a specific library, only to find out it performs like a dog in the real world, can be a massive setback. This is a situation where an ounce of prevention is worth a pound of the cure. You should always evaluate third-party modules before integrating them into your stack. Specific questions to ask:

- Does it cover your exact requirements or just come close?

- Is it a healthy project?

    - Does the maintainer have a good track record?

    - Is it well documented?

    - Does it have good test coverage?

    - How is the community (contributers, pull requests, etc)?

    - Is it under active development?

    - Are there lots of old issues and pull requests?

---

[4]   https://github.com/lincolnloop/django-layout ↗

- How does it perform?

  - How many database queries will it make?

  - Is it easy to cache?

- Does it have any impact on the rest of your applications?

- Does it have a license and is it compatible with your project?

Unmaintained and unstable third-party applications will quickly become a liability to your project. Once you dig through the source code you may discover that you only need a few lines to meet your needs. In that case, pulling in a new dependency might be overkill. Don't be afraid to copy the techniques you learn and adopt them to your project-specific needs.

WATCHING PERFORMANCE

Out of the box, Django doesn't give us much insight into what's happening during the request/response cycle. You'll want to add some functionality to see the performance characteristics of your pages during development. Django Debug Toolbar[5] is the tool of choice for this work. It will give you a page overlay showing you lots of information including database queries, templates used, timing, and more.

[5]   http://django-debug-toolbar.readthedocs.org/ ↗

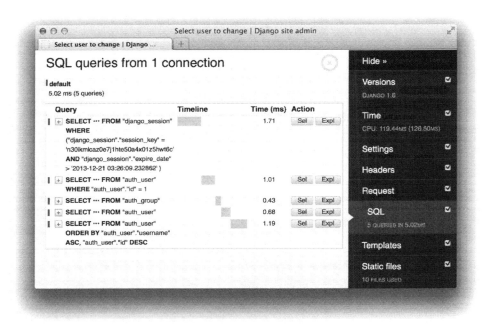

One issue with Debug Toolbar is that it doesn't work on AJAX or non-HTML requests. `django-debug-panel`[6] is an add-on that works around the limitation by displaying the Debug Toolbar in Chrome's web inspector with the help of a browser plugin.

If you prefer working in a console, you may find `django-devserver`[7] more to your liking. It is a `runserver` replacement that will show you similar information, but dumped out to the console instead of the browser.

Whichever tool you choose, the information you want to get at is the same. In order to efficiently optimize your code, you need quick answers to the following questions:

[6]   https://github.com/recamshak/django-debug-panel
[7]   https://github.com/dcramer/django-devserver

- How many SQL queries ran?

- What was the cumulative time spent in the database?

- What individual queries ran and how long did each one take?

- What code generated each query?

- What templates were used to render the page?

- How does a warm/cold cache affect performance? *Hint: use your settings to toggle the cache*

WHERE TO OPTIMIZE

DATABASE OPTIMIZATION

In almost every dynamic web application, the database is the performance bottleneck. It frequently needs to access information from the disks (the slowest part of a modern computer) and performs expensive in-memory calculation for complex queries. Minimizing both the number of queries and the time they need to run is a sure-fire way to speed up your application. We can attack this problem from a number of different angles, and there are usually a lot of low- hanging fruit for easy optimization. The following recommendations are presented from easiest to most difficult. You can work your way down the list until you reach your desired efficiency.

REDUCE QUERY COUNTS

Django's ORM makes it trivial to query and retrieve information from your database. A side effect is that it hides a lot of complexity, making it easy to write code that triggers lots and lots of queries. Even a seemingly innocuous template change can add tens (or even hundreds) of queries to a single response. In a complex application, it's easy to build a view which makes hundreds or even thousands of queries to the database. While you might be able to get away with this on a low traffic site, pages like this are a no-go on high-traffic sites. They'll crush even the beefiest database server under moderate load.

The good news is that by leveraging some of the advanced features of Django's ORM, it's possible to drop that number to 20 queries or less.

The first and simplest reduction is to look for places where `select_related` and `prefetch_related` can be used. These queryset methods come in handy when you know you'll be traversing foreign key relationships after the initial lookup. For example:

```python
# one query to post table
post = Post.objects.get(slug='this-post')
# one query to author table
name = post.author.name
```

This code makes two queries to the database. Once to fetch the post and another to fetch the author. A `select_related` can halve the queries by fetching the author object during the initial lookup.

```python
post = (Post.objects.select_related('author')
                    .get(slug='this-post'))
```

Saving one query isn't a big deal, but these queries usually stack up. Let's look at the following view and template:

```
post_list = Post.objects.all()
```

```
{% for post in post_list %}
  {{ post.title }}
  By {{ post.author.name }}
  in {{ post.category.name }}
{% endfor %}
```

This will do two queries on every loop iteration (author and category). In a list of 20 posts, we can drop the queries from 41 to 1:

```
post_list = (Post.objects.all()
                .select_related('author',
                                'category'))
```

This will use JOINs to lookup all the necessary data in a single query. There are rare scenarios where a JOIN will be more expensive than multiple queries so make sure you are keeping an eye on the total SQL time during this process. If you drop a couple queries, but your overall time goes up, it's probably better to keep the extra queries. The only caveat is that a database round-trip over the network in production is probably longer than localhost on your laptop.

select_related has a complementary method, prefetch_related which will allow you to do lookups in the other direction (getting all parents for a given child). The ORM can't collapse these lookups into a single query, but it will still result in a massive reduction in the overall query count.

Django's documentation on both `select_related` and `prefetch_related` is great and worth a review if you're feeling a little fuzzy on the subject:

- http://django.me/select-related ↗
- http://django.me/prefetch-related ↗

All of a view's queries are available in the SQL panel of Django Debug Toolbar. You can use it to identify places where a related lookup will help. Look for repeated queries that take the form of a SELECT with a WHERE clause on `id`. For example:

```
SELECT ... FROM blog_author WHERE id=8;
```

Simply track this query back to its source and sprinkle a `select_related` on it to make a huge dent in your total query count.

Sometimes, however, you'll add a `prefetch_related` method and the additional queries don't go away. Instead, you'll end up adding a query. Two things could be working against you in this case. First, make sure you aren't doing the additional lookups manually:

```
post = Post.objects.get(slug='this-post')
author = Author.objects.get(pk=post.author_id)
```

You'll also see this if you are putting additional filtering on the related queryset. For example:

```
post = (Post.objects.prefetch_related('tags')
                    .get(slug='this-post'))
```

```
# no extra queries
all_tags = post.tags.all()

# triggers additional query
active_tags = post.tags.filter(is_active=True)
```

In some scenarios it will be cheaper to take advantage of the cached query and do the additional filtering in memory:

```
active_tags = [tag for tag in all_tags if tag.is_active]
```

Also note the `Prefetch` object[8] added in Django 1.7 which gives you even more control over how `prefetch_related` works by letting you perform additional filtering on the related query.

While you are reviewing your queries, make sure all the queries are actually needed to render the view. Over time, it's possible to accumulate queries that aren't even used. Take this opportunity to axe them.

In general, this is easy work and on an un-optimized code base, this technique can help you drop well over 50% of the total queries.

REDUCE QUERY TIME

Once we have as few queries as possible, we want to make the remaining queries faster. Django Debug Toolbar comes to the rescue again. It will show us the slowest queries for any given page.

---

[8]   https://docs.djangoproject.com/en/1.7/ref/models/queries/#prefetch-objects

When you see a query that stands out as slow (greater than 50ms), check for the following issues:

MISSING INDEX

Adding indexes to a table is trivial, but figuring out where to add them can be a little challenging. If you're working with a really small dataset locally, you'll never see the issue because your RDBMS can scan the table quickly. This is one good reason to test with data that approximates what you have in production.

The main place a missing index will hurt performance is when the `WHERE` clause is used on a non-indexed column on a large table. Use the `EXPLAIN` statement to get some insight into what's happening under the hood. Django Debug Toolbar makes this accessible to you with the click of a button in the SQL panel. `EXPLAIN` output tends to be pretty verbose and complex, but there are a few simple clues you can look for.

In PostgreSQL, you are looking for places that `Seq Scan` is used instead of `Index Scan` and the "actual" rows is a really big number. In MySQL, look for places where the `key` and `possible_keys` columns are `NULL` and `rows` is a really big number. In both these scenarios, you can probably make gains by adding an index on the column(s) referenced in the `WHERE` clause. To add the index, simply add `db_index=True` to the field's definition in `models.py`.

If you frequently filter on multiple columns together, the `index_together`[9] model `Meta` option can be a huge improvement as

---

[9] https://docs.djangoproject.com/en/dev/ref/models/options/#index-together ↗

well. Just remember, however, that the ordering matters. Your index needs to be in the same order the fields are referenced in your SQL and filters otherwise your database can't use it.

In most cases, adding column indexes is an easy performance win. There are a few caveats though. First, test and verify that adding the index actually makes the query faster. In some cases, the database's query planner will not use an index if it can perform the query faster by other means. You should see an immediate drop in the query time once the index is added. Also keep in mind that indexes are not free. They need to be updated on every write to the database. If you have a write-heavy application, you'll want to investigate the performance impact. On read-heavy loads, adding the index is almost always a win.

EXPENSIVE TABLE JOINS

Joins aren't inherently bad, but sometimes they can result in very poor performance. If you see a slow query with a large `JOIN` clause, see if you can rewrite it so fewer joins are necessary. It usually requires some trial and error to find the ideal query structure, so don't be shy about opening up a console and testing the raw SQL. Use the `timing` flag in Postgres and profiler in MySQL to see the query times. In some cases, two queries may perform much better than one; you can get the `ids` from the first query and pass them into the second query:

```
tag_ids = (Post.objects.all()
                        .values_list('id', flat=True)
                        .distinct())
tags = Tag.objects.filter(id__in=tag_ids)
```

TOO MANY RESULTS

Be careful not to run unbounded queries. It's easy to have a `.all()` that works fine on your development machine, but against a production database returns thousands of results. Limit your queries using `queryset[:20]` (where 20 is the maximum results returned) or use pagination where appropriate.

COUNTS

Database counts are notoriously slow. Avoid them whenever possible. A common cause is Django's pagination, but custom paginators are available that don't require a full page count. In many cases, it isn't important to know the exact number of objects and the query can be avoided.

Another common source of counts is the anti-pattern:

```
posts = Post.objects.all()
if posts.count() > 0:
    # do something
```

Change these to use the much more performant `.exists()`:

```
posts = Post.objects.all()
if posts.exists():
    # do something
```

If all you need is an approximate count, there are a few hacks to get a recent (but not current) count out of the database without incurring the overhead. Take, for example, the following query in Postgres:

```
db=# \timing
Timing is on.
db=# SELECT COUNT(*) FROM image_thumbs;
 count
--------
 479099
(1 row)

Time: 8391.118 ms
db=# SELECT reltuples FROM pg_class
db=# WHERE relname = 'image_thumbs';
 reltuples
-----------
    475981
(1 row)

Time: 112.018 ms
```

That's a whopping 98% reduction in query time for a count that, in this case, is accurate within 1%. How about a similar technique in MySQL?

```
db> SELECT count(*) FROM image_thumbs;
+----------+
| count(*) |
+----------+
```

```
|   2759931 |
+-----------+
1 row in set (2.15 sec)

db> SELECT table_rows FROM information_schema.tables
    -> WHERE table_schema = DATABASE()
    -> AND table_name="image_thumbs";
+-------------+
| table_rows  |
+-------------+
|   2843604   |
+-------------+
1 row in set (0.10 sec)
```

The accuracy you'll get from these will vary, but in many cases, after a few hundred records, the exact number is not important and a rough estimate will do.

GENERIC FOREIGN KEYS

Generic foreign keys are a really cool feature in Django that lets you link arbitrary objects together and easily access them via the ORM. Unfortunately for optimization, they hide the fact that they unleash some nasty queries on your database to make it all work. Whenever possible, just avoid them. If for some reason you can't, keep in mind they will probably be an area that requires heavy caching early on.

EXPENSIVE MODEL METHODS

A common MVC practice is to build "fat models" that have methods for frequently used properties on an object. Often these methods do a number of database queries and package them up as a single property that is convenient for re-use elsewhere. If the properties are accessed more than once per request, you can optimize them with memoization[10]. The nice thing about this technique is that the cache only lives for the length of the request/response cycle so you're well protected from issues with the data becoming stale. Here's a simple example:

```python
from django.utils.functional import cached_property


class TheModel(models.Model):
    ...
    @cached_property
    def expensive(self):
        # expensive computation of result
        return result
```

RESULTS ARE TOO LARGE

For many applications, the cost of shipping the bits from your database to your application server is trivial. If, however, your models have fields that store sufficiently large amounts of data, it could be slowing down the transfer. Django provides a few queryset methods to work around this. `defer` and `only` return model objects while `values` and `values_list` return a list of dictionaries and tuples, respectively.

```python
# retrieve everything but the `body` field
posts = Post.objects.all().defer('body')

# retrieve only the `title` field
posts = Post.objects.all().only('title')
```

[10]   http://en.wikipedia.org/wiki/Memoization ↗

```python
# retrieve a list of {'id': id} dictionaries
posts = Post.objects.all().values('id')

# retrieve a list of (id,) tuples
posts = Post.objects.all().values_list('id')

# retrieve a list of ids
posts = Post.objects.all().values_list('id',
                                        flat=True)
```

TIP

values and *values_list* *bypass the process of initializing your Python model objects altogether. If you never intend to access methods or related fields, these methods are going to be more efficient and can shave off some unnecessary Python processing time.*

QUERY CACHING

The next place to look for performance gains is to remove duplicate queries via caching. For many workloads, a generic query cache will give you the biggest gains with the lowest effort. A query cache effectively sits in between the ORM and the database storing, fetching, and invalidating its cache automatically. Custom caching code is going to be more efficient, but it comes at a cost.

1. Humans have to write it. Humans are expensive and error-prone.

2. Cache invalidation is one of the hard problems in computer science.

There are a couple of good (well-tested, well-used) options in the Django ecosystem including Johnny Cache[11] and Cache Machine[12]. We found Johnny Cache to be the easiest to implement and it has proven stable for us under heavy workloads.

Johnny Cache appears pretty magical at first so its worth understanding what's happening under the hood (a good practice in general).

Johnny Cache works via a custom middleware. This middleware captures requests and puts the results of any database reads into the cache (Memcached or Redis). Future requests will check for queries stored in the cache and use them instead of hitting the database. Those queries are cached forever and key-based invalidation is used to keep it fresh. If Johnny Cache intercepts a write to a specific table, it updates a key invalidating all the cached queries for that table. It's a heavy-handed approach, but it guarantees your cache hits are always valid. Not having to worry about cache invalidation is a good thing.

Astute readers may have identified a problem with this approach – it is tied to the request/response cycle. One-off scripts, management commands, and background tasks won't invalidate the cache by default. Luckily, that can be fixed by adding this to your project's `__init__.py`:

[11] https://johnny-cache.readthedocs.org/en/latest/ ↗

[12] https://cache-machine.readthedocs.org/en/latest/ ↗

```
import johnny.cache
johnny.cache.enable()
```

This is the dividing line between the low hanging fruit of database optimization and the bigger guns. Make sure you've reviewed everything above this line before going any further. It's possible to handle massive amounts of traffic without any more special tricks. But if you're in a situation where the database still can't keep up, the following techniques may help. They're more work but can be effective for heavier workloads.

READ-ONLY REPLICAS

If your workload is read-heavy, adding more database servers can help distribute the load. Add a replica by using the replication mechanisms provided by your database. Django's multi-database and router support[13] will let you push all (or some) read traffic to the replica database.

RAW QUERIES

Django's ORM is flexible, but it can't do everything. Sometimes dropping to raw SQL can help you massage a particularly poor performing query into one that is more performant. Look into the `raw` method, or executing custom SQL, in the Django docs[14].

---

[13] https://docs.djangoproject.com/en/dev/topics/db/multi-db/ ↗

[14] https://docs.djangoproject.com/en/dev/topics/db/sql/#performing-raw-queries ↗

DENORMALIZATION

For joins that are a necessity, but too slow or not possible, some columns can be copied from the source table to the table needing the join. Effectively, this is caching data inside the database and along with it come all the typical caching problems. Writes for that table are now doubled because they need to update every table that includes a denormalized field. Additionally, extra care needs to be taken to make sure that all the values stay in sync.

ALTERNATE DATA STORES

We are big fans of the RDBMS. They are well suited for many different workloads and have first-class support in Django. With Postgres' hstore/json support[15], you can even do schemaless data better than many "NoSQL" data stores[16].

There are scenarios, however, where an alternative database can complement a RDBMS acting as the primary storage. The most common example of this is pushing data into Elasticsearch or Solr for their full-text search capabilities. Another NoSQL database you'll find hiding behind many high performance sites is Redis. Not only is it incredibly fast, but it also offers some unique data structures that can be leveraged to do things that are difficult or expensive in a RDBMS. Here are a couple write-ups that provide good examples of Redis complementing a RDBMS:

[15] http://www.postgresql.org/docs/9.3/static/functions-json.html ↗

[16] http://obartunov.livejournal.com/175235.html ↗

- Simon Willison's Redis Tutorial [17]

- Scaling SQL with Redis by David Cramer [18]

> ## *TIP*
>
> *Adding services in production isn't free. As developers, we often overlook this, but systems require support, configuration, monitoring, backup, etc. Keep in mind the maintenance burden and always think of your sysadmins!*

SHARDING

If you require database sharding, you're probably in the 0.1% of websites that need it. Save this until you are absolutely 100% sure it's the best option. Sharding lets you partition your data across multiple databases at the expense of auto-incrementing primary keys and foreign keys across those databases (among other things). It might be necessary if your database can't keep up with write traffic or the dataset is simply too large for the available RAM. Details on sharding are beyond the scope of this book, but if you happen to be in the 0.1% that needs it, there are many good resources online:

[17]

https://web.archive.org/web/20101227092136/http://simonwillison.net/static/2010/redis-tutorial/ ⁄

[18] http://cramer.io/2014/05/12/scaling-sql-with-redis/ ⁄

- Sharding Your Database (Heroku) [19]

- Why You Don't Want to Shard (Percona) [20]

- Scaling Pinterest presentation [21]

- Scaling Instagram presentation [22]

- Sharding IDs at Instagram [23]

- Example Sharding Tools (Disqus) [24]

TEMPLATE OPTIMIZATION

Django templates are the second biggest pain point in the stack. Switching to Jinja2 is an option for faster rendering. It will alleviate some of the pain, but also bring some new challenges and even with Jinja2, it's likely template rendering will still be the second slowest part of your stack. Instead we use caching to remove as much of the template rendering as possible from each response.

[19] http://www.craigkerstiens.com/2012/11/30/sharding-your-database/ ↗

[20] http://www.mysqlperformanceblog.com/2009/08/06/why-you-dont-want-to-shard/ ↗

[21] http://lanyrd.com/2013/qconsf/scrdgq/ ↗

[22] http://lanyrd.com/2012/airbnb-mike-krieger/srrzg/ ↗

[23] http://instagram-engineering.tumblr.com/post/10853187575/sharding-ids-at-instagram ↗

[24] https://github.com/disqus/sharding-example ↗

RUSSIAN DOLL CACHING

A favorite technique of ours, Russian doll caching, received some attention in the Ruby on Rails world due to a blog post from Basecamp founder, David Heinemeier Hansson[25]. The concept works very well in Django too. Basically, we nest cache calls with different expirations. Since the whole template won't expire simultaneously, only bits and pieces need to be rendered on any given request.

In practice it looks something like this:

```
{% cache MIDDLE_TTL "post_list" request.GET.page %}
  {% include "inc/post/header.html" %}
  <div class="post-list">
  {% for post in post_list %}
    {% cache LONG_TTL "post_teaser_" post.id post.last_modified %}
      {% include "inc/post/teaser.html" %}
    {% endcache %}
  {% endfor %}
  </div>
{% endcache %}
```

First, you'll notice the `MIDDLE_TTL` and `LONG_TTL` variables there. We pre-define a few sensible cache timeout values in the settings and pass them into the templates via a context processor. This lets us tweak the caching behavior site-wide from a central location. If you aren't sure where to start, we've been happy with 10 minutes (short), 30 minutes (medium),

---

[25] How Basecamp Next Got to Be So Damn Fast... (http://signalvnoise.com/posts/3112-how-basecamp-next-got-to-be-so-damn-fast-without-using-much-client-side-ui ↗) and follow-up posts, How Key Based Expiration Works (http://signalvnoise.com/posts/3113-how-key-based-cache-expiration-works ↗) and The Performance Impact of Russian Doll Caching (https://signalvnoise.com/posts/3690-the-performance-impact-of-russian-doll-caching ↗).

one hour (long), and 7 days (forever) on read-heavy, content-driven sites. On very high- traffic sites, even much lower values will relieve burden from your app servers.

The Russian doll technique comes in as we nest these calls from shortest expiration to longest expiration. The outside of the loop will expire more frequently, but it will not need to fetch every item in the loop on expiration. Instead, many of these will still be cached and fast.

Next let's analyze how the cache keys are built. On the outside cache fragment, we include the page number that was passed in as a URL parameter. This ensures the list is not reused across each page where the cache is used. Another thing to consider for object list caches is any filtering that is done on the list between pages (but sharing the same template). You may need to include a `category.id` or some other distinguishing characteristic.

The inner cache key uses key-based expiration. This is a great way to handle the difficulty of cache invalidation. We timestamp our models with a last modified date that gets updated on save, and use that date in our cache key. As long as the date hasn't changed, we can cache this fragment forever. If the date changes, Django will look for the object at a different cache key and miss, re-caching the object with the new key. There isn't a risk of overflowing the cache because "least recently used" (LRU) keys are flushed if additional space is needed.

CUSTOM CACHE TEMPLATE TAG

Django ships with a basic `cache` template tag, but we want some additional functionalities, so we often extend it with our own custom tag.

First, we want a convenience method to invalidate and reset all the cached HTML fragments for an entire page. This is a lifesaver for supporting your editorial team on publishing websites and is a big help to developers/support/admins when they are called to troubleshoot. Instead of telling them to wait and refresh the page in 1/5/20 minutes when the cache expires, they can simply generate a "fresh" page by appending a magic query parameter to the URL. You can even hit this magic URL from directly within your code to do a proactive cache flush in response to specific actions in your application.

Here is the relevant snippet to handle the invalidation:

```python
class CacheNode(template.Node):
    bust_param = 'flush-the-cache'
    ...
    def needs_cache_busting(self, request):
        bust = False
        if request.GET and (self.bust_param in request.GET):
            bust = True
        return bust

    def render(self, context):
        ...
        value = cache.get(cache_key)
        if self.needs_cache_busting(request) or value is None:
            value = self.nodelist.render(context)
            cache.set(cache_key, value, expire_time)
        return value
```

Another issue you'll encounter is the simultaneous expiration of multiple cache keys. When you throw a bunch of content into cache with the same timeout, it is all going to expire at the same time. Over time, the problem tends to get worse as expiration times start to synchronize. Your cache server ends up on a roller-coaster doing lots of sets at repeating intervals, resulting in the thundering herd problem[26]. This can be mitigated by applying jitter to your cache expiration times. Here is a simplified example to apply a +/-20% jitter:

```
def jitter(num, variance=0.2):
    min_num = num * (1 - variance)
    max_num = num * (1 + variance)
    return randint(min_num, max_num)
```

A full version of the custom template tag code can be found as a Gist on GitHub (https://gist.github.com/ipmb/cb0c667ee4a7acd6c4f8 ↗).

DO SLOW WORK LATER

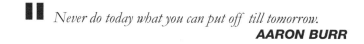 *Never do today what you can put off till tomorrow.*
AARON BURR

Getting Django views to complete in less than 200ms doesn't leave a lot of overhead for extra computation. Modern web applications commonly have views that need to make calls to external services or perform heavy-duty processing on data or files. The best way to make those views

---

[26]   http://en.wikipedia.org/wiki/Thundering_herd_problem ↗

fast is to push the slow work to a job queue. In the Python world, Celery is the job queue of choice. Simpler ones exist, but beyond a certain scale, Celery should be the one you reach for since you'll probably want some of its more advanced features.

Celery requires a separate message queuing service to transport job information from your application to the workers. For low volumes, Redis is good enough to act as a queue service and, if it's already in use, helps keep your infrastructure simple. For sites with more intensive needs, RabbitMQ tends to be the queue of choice.

Good candidates for background tasks that can be pushed to Celery are:

- Third-party API calls

- Sending email

- Heavy computational tasks (video processing, number crunching, etc.)

In some cases, you'll want to prioritize jobs. Tasks that have a user waiting for a result are more important than run-of-the-mill system maintenance tasks. For these scenarios, it makes sense to split your work into multiple queues. Jobs on your high-priority queue should be picked up immediately, while it's ok for your low-priority queue to wait from time to time. This is easy enough to accomplish by modifying the number of workers assigned to each queue or the size of the servers that house those workers. It is one of the other places where auto-scaling can come in handy.

A couple tips on structuring your tasks:

Do not use stateful objects such as models as arguments to the tasks. This reasoning is twofold. One, you don't know when the task is going to execute. There is a risk of the database changing by the time a model object is picked up by a worker. It's better to send a primary key and fetch a fresh copy of the object from the database in the task. The other reason is the serialization process required to push the task and its arguments on the queue. For complex objects this process can be expensive and a source of problematic issues.

Keep your tasks small and don't hesitate to have one task trigger more tasks. By breaking up long-running jobs into small atomic tasks, you can spread them across more workers/CPUs and churn through them faster. (There is some overhead to creating tasks, so don't go too crazy here.) Another benefit is that you can quickly restart and kill-off worker processes safely. A worker will not gracefully stop until is has completed its current task so keeping tasks small will make your deployments faster.

!WARNING!

If you are creating an object in the database and then immediately creating a task that depends on it, you can get into a race condition between the the database transaction committing and the task getting picked up by an available worker. If the worker wins, your task will fail. This can be worked around by delaying the task execution for a few seconds or the django-transaction-hooks [27] library.

For tips on advanced Celery usage, Daniel Gouldin's talk, *Using Celery with Social Networks* [28] from DjangoCon 2012 is a great resource.

Scheduled tasks are another opportunity to cut back on hefty views. Good candidates for scheduled tasks are administration reports, cleaning up dead records in the database, or fetching data from third-party services. Since we're already using Celery, the "beat" functionality [29] is a good option to manage these tasks.

Celery beat lets your developers easily add new scheduled tasks with Python functions and Django settings instead of building out custom management commands. Defining cronjobs usually requires a context switch to the configuration management tools, or worse, manually setting

---

[27] https://django-transaction-hooks.readthedocs.org/ ↗

[28] http://celery.readthedocs.org/en/latest/userguide/periodic-tasks.html ↗

[29] http://lanyrd.com/2012/djangocon-us/sxbyb/ ↗

it up on a server and then forgetting about it. Additionally, Celery has support for things that `cron` does not like - retrying failed tasks and finer grained schedules.

Finally, you should already be monitoring Celery tasks for failures, so your periodic task monitoring is already there.

For stacks that aren't already using Celery or aren't sold on the benefits, good ol' Unix `cron` is certainly a viable option.

FRONT-END OPTIMIZATIONS

It's easy to get lost in the performance of your back-end services, but important to remember that they only paint one piece of the end-user's experience. We've seen Django sites that can render pages in less than 200ms on the back-end, but require 7 seconds to load into the browser. Entire books have been written on the topic of front-end performance[30], so we'll just hit the topics that overlap with Django.

To measure your front-end performance and see where it can be improved, look at YSlow[31] and Google's PageSpeed[32]. They are both offered as browser plugins that give you immediate data on page load similar to Django Debug Toolbar.

---

[30] High Performance Websites (http://shop.oreilly.com/product/9780596529307.do ↗)

[31] https://developer.yahoo.com/yslow/ ↗

[32] https://developers.google.com/speed/pagespeed/ ↗

MINIMIZING CSS & JAVASCRIPT

In some ways, you can think of CSS and JavaScript files like database queries:

- Fewer is better.

- Smaller is better.

- They should be cached whenever possible.

To make this happen, you'll need a tool that can collect, concatenate, minify, and version your static files. The result is a payload that not only small and fast over the wire, but can be cached forever in the browser.

A number of solid libraries in the Django ecosystem are up to handling this task including `django-pipeline`[33], `django-compressor`[34], and `webassets`[35]. Our current preference is Pipeline. It provides all the necessary functionality and doesn't add any significant overhead to the template rendering.

If your site has a large JavaScript code base, it may make more sense to relegate this task to front-end build tools where you can take advantage of tools like Require.js[36] or Browserify[37].

---

[33] https://django-pipeline.readthedocs.org/en/latest/ ↗

[34] http://django-compressor.readthedocs.org/en/latest/ ↗

[35] http://webassets.readthedocs.org/en/latest/ ↗

[36] http://requirejs.org/ ↗

[37] http://browserify.org/ ↗

COMPRESS IMAGES

People put a lot of focus on JavaScript and CSS optimization, but often it only shaves a few kilobytes off of the first page load. In contrast, photo-heavy sites can save *megabytes* per page load by optimizing their images and thumbnails.

Static assets are easy enough to optimize locally via `pngcrush` or similar tools prior to checking them into version control. If your users are uploading images, that's another story. As part of your thumbnailing process, consider running them through an optimizer like the one included in `easy-thumbnails`[38]. It's not uncommon to cut down the size by 50% or more with this technique.

---

[38]   http://easy-thumbnails.readthedocs.org/en/latest/ref/optimize/ ↗

SERVE ASSETS FROM A CDN

Leveraging a CDN like those provided by Amazon Cloudfront or Rackspace/Akamai is not only going to improve performance for your end-users, but also reduce traffic and complexity on your servers. By pushing these assets to a CDN, you can let your servers focus on serving dynamic data and leave static files to your CDN.

Getting files into your CDN isn't always a straightforward process, however. Some of the static file compression tools like `django-compressor` and `django-pipeline` already support custom storage backends, while others will require extra steps to get your files to a CDN. Another approach is to serve your static files directly from your app servers and set it up as a dynamic origin for your CDN (Amazon Cloudfont has this capability). There are a number of options for static file serving in your stack including uWSGI[39] and WSGI middleware[40].

Third-party storage back-ends also exist that will let you send files directly to your CDN, but that comes with its own challenges.

FILE UPLOADS

With a single app server, uploading files is a pretty trivial process. You can store, manipulate, and serve them from the local filesystem. Once you start adding app servers, however, this approach becomes problematic. You can create a shared volume via NFS or use something more robust like GlusterFS or Ceph, but for most sites, commercial offerings like

[39] http://uwsgi-docs.readthedocs.org/en/latest/StaticFiles.html ↗

[40] http://whitenoise.evans.io/ ↗

Amazon S3 or Rackspace Cloud Files are going to be easier and relatively inexpensive options. As a bonus, you'll get to use their CDN as part of the package.

Once file uploads are moved off the local disk, manipulating them (e.g. thumbnailing or optimizing images) becomes painfully slow. The server needs to download the image from the remote storage, manipulate it, then upload the result. On a page with 20 thumbnails, these network round-trips add up quickly and kill performance.

We take a two-fold approach to this problem. Common operations are predefined and done upfront. In the common case of image thumbnails, we define all the common sizes in the Django settings. On upload, task(s) are sent to Celery to pre-generate and upload those thumbnails in the background. As a failsafe, we maintain the ability for thumbnails to be generated on-the-fly from a template tag. This ensures users will never see broken thumbnails in the event of the first request happening before the queued task completes.

TESTING

A good test suite is a strong indicator of a healthy code base. It lets your team deploy with confidence instead of nerve-wracking scrambles to fix unexpected regressions.

Our approach to testing is pragmatic; we don't buy wholesale into any one particular philosophy. The priority is to get test coverage on the parts of your code that are the most difficult, most important, and most likely to break. 100% test coverage is a valiant goal, but it doesn't guarantee your code is bug free and is rarely an efficient use of development time.

AUTOMATED TESTING AND CONTINUOUS INTEGRATION

Tests are only good when they run and when developers know if they fail. Early on in your development process, you should have a continuous integration system in place that will run automated tests and health checks on your code base to ensure it's in good shape.

We typically use Jenkins CI [41] to run a number of checks on our code, including:

- Unit tests

- Code coverage

- PEP8/Linting

- Functional tests via Selenium

- Performance tests via Jmeter (discussed in Load Testing with Jmeter (page 108))

[41] http://jenkins-ci.org/ ↗

`django-discover-jenkins`[42] can help you get your project working with Jenkins quickly. It handles outputting unit test results in a format Jenkins can understand as well as providing coverage, pylint, and flake8 functionality.

TIP

Testing services such as Travis CI[43] are growing in popularity and make it simple to get started with continuous integration. As with any hosted service, you may be trading off a significant amount of flexibility for what types of data you can capture and how it is displayed.

So far, we've showed you how to get your site built and running efficiently on your development machine, but that's only half the battle. Launching a high performance Django website is impossible without a good server infrastructure. In the next section, we'll discuss the production deployment – moving the code off your laptop and onto well-tuned servers.

[42] https://django-discover-jenkins.readthedocs.org/en/latest/ ↗
[43] https://travis-ci.org/ ↗

THE DEPLOYMENT

CHAPTER 3
THE DEPLOYMENT

Deployment encompasses everything needed to make your code run on live servers, so getting it right is crucial to your site's stability. Bad deploys can bring your entire site down or, worse, leave lingering issues that take weeks or months before they rear their ugly heads. If your deployment process is a nerve-wracking experience complete with sweaty palms and crossed-fingers, you're doing it wrong. In this chapter, we'll focus less on your Django code and more on the supporting cast of critical services for a high performance site.

PREREQUISITES

There are a few prerequisites to stable deployments that are outside the scope of this book but lay a critical foundation for stability. We'll touch on them here, but if any of these concepts are new or unfamiliar, do your research before moving forward.

OPERATING SYSTEM

Unix/Linux based systems rule the land for Django deployment. Ubuntu is the preferred distribution amongst Django developers but there are many other valid options. Unless you have lots of experience working with another distribution, just choose Ubuntu. If you do look at another OS, make sure:

1. It uses current packages. If you can't easily use Python 2.7 or higher, choose another platform. CentOS/RHEL are notorious for being a version or two behind.

2. It will have security updates into the foreseeable future. We use Ubuntu LTS (Long Term Support) versions so we don't have to rebuild our servers every year or two.

CONFIGURATION MANAGEMENT

Reliable deployments are impossible without a stable homogeneous platform across all your servers. If they have divergent configurations or different software versions you're gonna have a bad time.

Configuration management lets you define what it means to be an "app server" and roll out new ones at will. There are lots of options in the configuration management space systems and the decision really comes down to experience and personal preference. Chef and Puppet have a lot of mind-share, but newer tools like Ansible and Salt are making headway. We have been using Salt for the last year and are very happy with it.

!WARNING!

Fabric [1] *is* **not** *a configuration management tool. Trying to use it as one will ultimately cause you heartache and pain. Fabric is an excellent choice for executing scripts in one or more remote systems, but that's only a small piece of the puzzle. Don't reinvent the wheel by building your own configuration management system on top of Fabric.*

PROCESS MANAGEMENT

As with configuration management, there are many options for making sure your services start when the server starts up, and get restarted in the event of a crash. We prefer to use the default OS tools (upstart, systemd, etc.) rather than adding another layer of software into the mix.

Alternatively, you may find these tools too limited or difficult to work with. In that case, daemontools[2], supervisord[3], or circus[4] may suit your needs better. Whatever you choose, this should be one part of your stack that never fails. If you find yourself fighting with it, consider choosing a different tool.

[1]   http://www.fabfile.org/ ↗

[2]   http://cr.yp.to/daemontools.html ↗

[3]   http://supervisord.org/ ↗

[4]   http://circus.readthedocs.org/ ↗

SHIPPING YOUR CODE

Shipping a new build usually requires a number of steps:

1. Checkout the latest code from version control

2. Update dependencies

3. Migrate database

4. Collect, compress, and push static files to CDN

5. Reload WSGI server

6. Restart background workers

As with the rest of the process, simplicity is the key to making deployments repeatable and reliable. You can simplify this multi-step process by scripting everything so it only requires a single click or command. Anything more complicated than one step is an opportunity for human error to creep into the process.

A remote execution framework is the right tool for this job. Salt has remote execution baked in so that's what we use, but Fabric is also a great option.

MULTIPLE REMOTE ENVIRONMENTS

Having multiple remote environments you can deploy to is a good idea for any website, but critical for large-scale operations. Non-production environments give your team a place to stage new features for feedback, QA builds before deployment, or test infrastructure changes without taking down production services. The number of environments you have depends on your work-flow, but plan on having at least two (staging/development and production).

As your production server farm gets larger, running an exact replica of its infrastructure becomes financially infeasible for development and testing. You can scale back both horizontally (fewer servers) and vertically (fewer

---

[5] http://uwsgi-docs.readthedocs.org/en/latest/articles/TheArtOfGracefulReloading.html ↗

resources per server), but try keep the same general server/service layout. Each separate environment should be completely isolated from the others, especially production. Your team needs to have confidence that they can break things in development without taking down production services.

Each environment should be as close to production as possible (settings, software, OS, etc.). There are few things more maddening for a developer than a bug that only shows up in production because of a lack of parity in the development environment. In your effort to reach environment parity, you'll hit places where it conflicts with the goal of environment isolation. For example, you'll definitely need to diverge in your third-party service configurations. You don't want your development environment processing payments or sending files to your production CDN. Always favor pure isolation over exact parity in that battle.

One problem with maintaining a good development environment is populating it with data. It's common to see people using a replica of the production database in development. If you're considering this approach, also consider a few major risks associated with it:

- Is your development environment as secure as production? Loosely monitored development machines are a common attack vector for black hats.

- Is it possible to send out emails or other notifications from your application? Having your development environment accidentally send out thousands of emails to your users is not only embarrassing, but could impact the business as well.

AVOIDING SINGLE POINTS OF FAILURE

Single points of failure are the sworn enemy of any good system administrator. In much the same way your server can withstand the loss of a single hard drive, your infrastructure should be able to withstand the loss of a server without catastrophic results.

Netflix has gone so far as to build a piece of software that randomly kills production systems to ensure high-availability and fault tolerance (aptly named, Chaos Monkey[6]). This is probably overkill for your site, but that thinking can get you in the right mindset for avoiding SPOFs (single points of failure). Mentally go down your stack and think about what would happen in the event of a lost server or service at every level.

The loss of a stateless service like an application server is usually easy to withstand, but the loss of production data can be catastrophic. Make sure you know every place that data (databases, user uploads, etc) is stored in your system and that it is backed up. See also, Backup *(page 94)*.

NOTE

As part of your planning, you'll want to determine if high availability is a business requirement. HA (high availability) is the process of automatically failing over when systems become unavailable without a service outage or manual intervention. Keep in mind that the cost of implementing HA often outweighs the cost of downtime.

[6]   http://techblog.netflix.com/2012/07/chaos-monkey-released-into-wild.html

Once you've worked your way through *your* stack, you'll want to consider your hosting provider and decide how to handle *their* outages. Take for example, Amazon EC2. Do you need to be able to withstand an availability zone going down? How about an entire region? What if all of Amazon goes down? Answering and documenting these questions early on will avoid a lot of confusion and panic in the event of a real catastrophe.

SERVER LAYOUT

By this point, you should have a good idea of how all the pieces of software work together. But how do they map out to physical/virtual servers? And what resources will those servers need? Let's look at each component, starting at the top of our stack and moving our way down.

LOAD BALANCER

Load balancers are simple traffic proxies and not extremely resource intensive. If you are hosting at a cloud provider such as Rackspace or Amazon, using their managed load balancer offering is often an inexpensive and easy way to go. Otherwise, a medium-sized virtual machine setup with Nginx or Haproxy can proxy a surprising amount of traffic and still be mostly idle. Network throughput is the thing you need to keep an eye out for on these machines.

WEB ACCELERATOR

Your web accelerator can live in a few different places. It may do double duty as your load balancer and live on that box. It can be on a box of its own, or it can live on the same servers as your application. Putting it on your app servers means they won't all share a cache which will lower the cache hit rate, but it also gives you more redundancy. Losing one simply drops that app server out of the load balancer pool instead of taking down the entire website.

Wherever it lives, it will need good network throughput and lots of RAM to store the cached responses in memory.

APPLICATION

Your application layer is typically going to be limited by CPU and/or RAM and is the first layer you'll need to start scaling horizontally. A few smaller machines are preferable to a single massive machine for redundancy if one fails.

You'll run multiple WSGI workers so each machine can serve multiple requests simultaneously and take advantage of every processor core. The exact number depends on a number of factors. See uWSGI Tuning (page 70) for more info.

BACKGROUND WORKERS

Background workers are often CPU bound and should run on their own servers. Like application servers, a single server can run many workers.

They are also similar in that they are state-less and can easily be added and removed depending on workload.

CACHE

Your cache machines need RAM and lots of it. A dedicated cache machine is rarely CPU bound and the disk speed will have very little affect on its performance. It's hard to determine the right amount of RAM upfront, but it's easy to see when you don't have enough. With too little RAM, your cache will start doing LRU (least recently used) cache evictions. If you see the cache eviction rate going up, it means your cache server could take advantage of more RAM.

Another consideration on caches is their network throughput. It may become a bottleneck before the RAM. If the network is becoming saturated, Django can be configured to distribute traffic across multiple servers. See CACHES *(page 74)* for more.

DATABASE

When spec'ing hardware for your database, don't skimp. The database is usually the beefiest box in the server farm. The two most important things for a database are fast disks and lots of RAM.

A good rule of thumb is to have enough RAM to keep your entire dataset in memory. If you expect to have a 60GB database, spec out a box with at least 64GB of RAM. This will minimize the round-trips to disk to fetch data by letting your database cache all the data in memory.

Disk speed is important; buy the fastest disks you can afford. Fast hardware can defer expensive database optimizations, sometimes indefinitely. As Jeff Atwood says, "When does it make sense to throw hardware at a programming problem? As a general rule, I'd say almost *always*."[7] If SSDs are in the budget, use them.

If you are deploying to a virtual machine, keep in mind you'll be sharing physical disks with your neighbors. A common practice is to buy the largest virtual machine possible. Even if it has more RAM or CPU than you need, it usually guarantees you'll be the only one on the physical hardware. This protects you from noisy/misbehaving neighbors. An added benefit is that it will give you access to more internal network bandwidth as well.

A WORD ON AUTO SCALING

One of the promises of cloud computing is auto-scaling. As traffic to your site increases, new servers magically spin up to handle the load. When the traffic subsides, those servers get killed to save you money. Unfortunately, it's an idea that has been overmarketed and leads people to believe that it will make any old website scale to billions of users. That's pretty far from the truth, but there are a few places where auto-scaling can be effective.

Application servers are the perfect candidate for auto-scaling. They have no state (that lives in your database), they are all more or less identical, and it is easy to add/remove them to the load balancing pool on the fly. A typical auto-scaling rule will say that if some metric gets too high on your application servers (load, CPU, busy workers, etc.) then add another

[7]   http://blog.codinghorror.com/hardware-is-cheap-programmers-are-expensive/ ↗

server to the pool. When the load subsides, pull it out and destroy the server. For sites with bursty traffic, auto-scaling can be a real money-saver.

Job queue workers are another place where auto-scaling can be very effective.

Auto-scaling does not, however, work as well on stateful systems such as your database. It's possible to bring on extra database replicas to handle heavy read traffic, but bringing a new replica online is a time-consuming process with a large database and may require reconfiguring your application to utilize it.

One major risk with auto-scaling is simply pushing a problem farther down your stack. Remember, we want to keep as much traffic as we can in the higher layers of the stack for performance reasons. Adding application servers typically means more database traffic. If your database is already running hot, you'll just be throwing logs on the fire.

TUNING THE STACK

Once you've got your servers up and running and the software installed, you'll want to take full advantage of all the resources your server can muster. To really make things hum, you've got to make some adjustments under the hood.

DATABASE TUNING

Out of the box, Postgres and MySQL are not tuned for high performance. There are lots of knobs you can turn to improve performance and the exact settings are dependent on your workload. That being said, there are a few adjustments we can make up front to have a better starting point. Unless you're a skilled DBA (Database Administrator), the best bang for your buck is to give your database plenty of hardware, make these macro adjustments and then step back and let it do its thing.

POSTGRESQL

The major settings you need to change out of the gate are the memory resources Postgres is allowed to consume. Adjusting these will let it make full use of the RAM you have in the system.

- `shared_buffers` 25% of RAM up to 8GB

- `work_mem` (2x RAM) / max_connections

- `maintenance_work_mem` RAM / 16

- `effective_cache_size` RAM / 2

- `max_connections` less than 400

These numbers are pulled directly from Christophe Pettus' talk, *PostgreSQL when it's not your job*[8], an amazing resource on the topic of PostgreSQL configuration. Be sure to watch it or at the very least flip through his slides for more great tips.

[8]   http://lanyrd.com/2012/djangocon-europe/srpqz/ ↗

MYSQL

Percona has a slick configuration wizard[9] that should give you sane defaults for your `my.cnf`. Note that MySQL has fewer options to fine-tune memory usage than Postgres. To make full use of the RAM, set the following value:

- `innodb-buffer-pool-size` 80% of RAM

UWSGI TUNING

uWSGI has an overwhelming set of options to tweak its performance and behavior. Here are a few of the common ones we use:

- `processes`

  Determine the number of concurrent requests your server can handle. A good rule of thumb is to start with double the processor cores in the machine and go up until you approach maxing out the CPU or RAM. If you have other services such as memcached or Varnish on your applications servers, you'll want to start with fewer processes (number of cores + 1). Too many processes and you will see high CPU wait times as they all contend for CPU time. Too few and you'll be leaving resources idle, forcing requests to queue up and wait.

- `threads`

  If your application is thread-safe, adding threads can be a lightweight option to further increase concurrency. Use the `stats` option (see

---

[9] https://tools.percona.com/wizard ↗

below) and `uwsgitop` to determine the optimal number of processes and threads for your workload and available resources.

- `thunder-lock`

  This option will help uWSGI balance the load better amongst all the processes/threads. The uWSGI docs have a lengthy explanation[10] of what it does and why it is not the default behavior.

- `harakiri`

  The maximum number of seconds a worker can take to process a single request before it is killed off. This will help keep runaway tasks in check and prevent all the workers from getting tied up with long-running requests.

- `max-requests`

  Despite our best intentions, applications can leak memory over time. The correct way to handle it is to fix the memory leak at the source. As a stop-gap, however, you can tell uWSGI to respawn a worker after X requests, freeing up its memory. If you do decide to use this option, set it to a sufficiently high number so the server isn't doing extra work to respawn workers every few minutes.

- `post-buffering`

  The max size of an HTTP request body in bytes (usually a file upload) that will go into memory. Larger requests will be saved to a temporary file on disk. Setting it to 4096 means that file uploads

---

[10] http://uwsgi-docs.readthedocs.org/en/latest/articles/SerializingAccept.html

cannot bloat the memory of a process by more than 4MB as they are being read.

- `stats`

  This option will publish statistics about the uWSGI process, including number of requests, average response time, memory usage per worker and more. It can use TCP (e.g., 127.0.0.1:1717) or a Unix domain (e.g., `/tmp/stat.sock`) socket. You can `pip install uwsgitop` for a nice text-based UI or push them into your metrics system for later analysis.

- `auto-procname`

  A nicer human-readable process name that shows the purpose of each process, e.g. http, router, master.

- `procname-prefix-spaced`

  Adds a prefix to the process names. Useful if you are hosting multiple sites on the same machine.

EMPEROR MODE

When running multiple sites or applications on a single server, uWSGI's emperor mode makes it easy to spin up new sites similar to Nginx/Apache's `sites-enabled` functionality. In the uWSGI world, each site is referred to as a vassal.

The emperor takes over all process management of individual vassals. Adding a file starts a new vassal, and deleting the file will kill the vassal process on the fly. Editing or touching the file gracefully reloads the vassal

[11] http://docs.gunicorn.org/en/latest/install.html#async-workers ↗

[12] https://glyph.twistedmatrix.com/2014/02/unyielding.html ↗

[13] http://lincolnloop.com/blog/architecting-realtime-applications/ ↗

process. It will even monitor and respawn processes that have died unexpectedly.

To enable emperor mode, simply add the following line to the `uwsgi` section of your configuration file:

```
emperor = /etc/uwsgi/vassals-enabled
```

Now any `.ini` file you drop into `/etc/uwsgi/vassals-enabled` will automatically be read and the main (emperor) uWSGI instance will start up a new vassal instance.

TUNING DJANGO

Like the rest of our stack, some of the defaults in Django are suboptimal for high-traffic websites. Here are a few you'll want to check.

CACHES

There are really only two viable options here, Memcached or Redis. If you are using Memcached be sure to choose the `pylibmc` library for the best performance and stability. There are a few third-party libraries for Redis, but `django-redis`[14] seems to be leading the pack at the moment.

Out of the box, when used properly, these cache back-ends can provide a massive performance boost. Unfortunately, they are also susceptible to a few issues when used on a larger scale.

---

[14]   http://niwibe.github.io/django-redis/

The first issue is the cache stampede (aka dog piling) problem[15]. Given enough application servers and users, a cache key expiration can flood your database and/or your cache server to refresh the key. Luckily, there's a simple package (actually just a single file) which solves this well. `django-newcache`, was originally written by Eric Florenzano, but you'll want to use a more recent fork[16] with updates for the current Django versions.

Another gotcha with Django's caching is that adding cache servers does not increase durability; it actually reduces it. Losing a cache service due to the server going down or network issues is a fatal error and will result in a "500 Server Error" being returned to the user. If you go from one to three cache servers, you are actually *increasing* the chance of failure. You should consider whether you want a cache server going down to take your site down with it, or if you want your application to keep going and treat it as a cache miss. This will put more pressure on your database, but in the event of a transient issue, it may be better than serving error pages.

Unfortunately, the best way to work around this is to fork the Django cache backend. We released django-ft-cache[17] which offers this functionality by simply wrapping any memcached operations in a `try/except` block. Exceptions are caught so the request can continue, but logged so an administrator can take action if a server has failed.

Django docs:

---

[15]   http://en.wikipedia.org/wiki/Cache_stampede ↗

[16]   https://github.com/joshourisman/django-newcache ↗

[17]   https://github.com/lincolnloop/django-ft-cache ↗

https://docs.djangoproject.com/en/dev/ref/settings/#caches ↗

SESSION_ENGINE

The database is the default storage for sessions. Since we want to touch the database as little as possible, having every request hitting it is a no go. This is easy to swap out for a nice little performance boost.

The `cache` backend is a good option, especially if you are using Redis and it is configured to persist to disk.

The `cached_db` backend works well if you use Memcached, but want to ensure your sessions survive a cache restart. This backend will still hit the database, but far less than the default backend.

Another option is to use the `signed_cookies` backend, letting your clients store the data and pass it back with every request. There are some risks involved with this approach, so be sure to read up on the notes in the docs [18].

DATABASES

Django 1.6 added the option of persistent database connections. Prior to this, every request needed to renegotiate a connection to the database and tear it down upon completion. Before 1.6, the recommended approach was to setup a separate connection pooler, making this feature not only a win for performance, but also simplicity.

For backwards compatibility reasons this feature is off by default. You'll

---

[18] https://docs.djangoproject.com/en/dev/topics/http/sessions/#using-cookie-based-sessions ↗

want to add the `CONN_MAX_AGE` key to any database defined in your `DATABASES` setting. `300` is a good value to start with if you're unsure. That tells Django to hold open and reuse database connections for 5 minutes. `None` can also be used to recycle them indefinitely.

Django docs:

https://docs.djangoproject.com/en/dev/ref/settings/#databases ⬈

LOGGING

Django can log directly to a file via Python's logging module, but we recommend against it. It is a common source of file permissions issues, especially if you have developers or admins hopping on a server to inspect data via `manage.py shell`. If Django can't write to the log file it will crash on startup and hair-pulling will ensue.

Instead, output to `STDERR` and either have uWSGI log this to file using the `--logto` option, or pick up the output with your process manager (upstart, systemd, supervisor, etc.). A basic logging configuration to stream to the console looks like this:

```
LOGGING = {
    'version': 1,
    'disable_existing_loggers': False,
    'handlers': {
        'console': {
            'level': 'INFO',
            'class': 'logging.StreamHandler',
            'formatter': 'verbose',
        },
    },
    'formatters': {
        'verbose': {
```

```
        'format': (
            '%(asctime)s [%(process)d] [%(levelname)s] ' +
            'pathname=%(pathname)s lineno=%(lineno)s ' +
            'funcname=%(funcName)s %(message)s'),
        'datefmt': '%Y-%m-%d %H:%M:%S'
    },
    'simple': {
        'format': '%(levelname)s %(message)s',
    },
}
'loggers': {
    'django': {
        'handlers': ['console'],
    }
}
}
```

TIP

uWSGI has some pretty advanced logging options[19] that will let you stream its request logs and your application logs to different locations. You can even filter logs based on regular expressions.

Django logging docs:

https://docs.djangoproject.com/en/dev/topics/logging/#configuring-logging ↗

[19] http://uwsgi-docs.readthedocs.org/en/latest/Logging.html ↗

MIDDLEWARE_CLASSES

Be very careful with custom middleware. It's a code path that will execute on *every* request to the application, so make sure you know what each one is doing and avoid database queries in middleware whenever possible.

Django docs: https://docs.djangoproject.com/en/dev/ref/middleware/ ↗

GENERAL SECURITY

There's a handful of bits you can flip to make sure your site isn't vulnerable to exploits like clickjacking and XSS (Cross Site Scripting). The easiest way to enable all these is via the `django-secure` project[20]. Simply install it and run `manage.py checksecure` to verify your production installation. In some cases, your project requirements may not allow you to enable all of the security features. In that case, make sure you understand the trade-off, and that your reasoning has been documented for future developers. OWASP[21] is a great resource for understanding why all these options are important.

On the topic of security, make sure your administration interface is adequately protected. If it's open to the public, one weak admin password can take down your whole site. Treat it like any other internal service and don't leave it open on the public internet. See also, Protect internal services *(page 92)*.

---

[20] https://github.com/carljm/django-secure#readme ↗

[21] https://www.owasp.org ↗

WEB ACCELERATOR

Unlike some of the other services, Varnish won't "just work" out of the box. It requires configuration and also thought about how your application works and where you can take advantage of its caching. The end goal is to have Varnish serving as much of your traffic as possible, protecting the slower services that sit below it in the stack.

First, you need to determine what content can be shared between users. The simplest example is traffic that comes from anonymous (not logged in) users. You want Varnish to cache the response to any request from an anonymous user and serve it back to other anonymous users visiting the same URL.

Varnish uses a domain specific language called VCL (Varnish Configuration Language) that looks a lot like Perl or C. We'll only scratch the surface of it here, but they have extensive docs[22] and it's usually possible to find snippets that do what you want after a couple of Google searches. The default location for the Varnish configuration is `/etc/varnish/default.vcl`.

[22] https://www.varnish-cache.org/docs/4.0/users-guide/ ↗

TIP

Debugging your VCL configuration is not always a piece of cake. You may find the Varnish log function (`std.log("...")`) helpful to confirm the path a request/response takes through your configuration.

DEFINING BACKEND(S)

Before you dive into configuring how Varnish handles requests, you need to tell Varnish how to talk to your application servers ("backends" in VCL).

---

[23] https://www.varnish-cache.org/docs/4.0/whats-new/upgrading.html

Here's a simple example:

```
backend mysite {
    .host = "127.0.0.1";
    .port = "8080";
}
```

This block tells Varnish that our Django site is available at http://127.0.0.1:8080 ↗. Multiple backends can be defined and load balanced using directors[24].

VCL_RECV *SUBROUTINE*

Varnish uses "subroutines" to allow you to customize how it behaves during different stages of a request/response cycle. The first one we'll use is `vcl_recv`. It is called when a request is received, and is used to modify it before it does a cache lookup.

Varnish caches responses based on the URL and the contents of the headers defined by the `Vary` header. A typical Django request may vary on `Accept-Encoding` and `Cookie`. For anonymous requests, the cookies rarely matter (and are often set by third-party analytics platforms). You'll improve your hit rate greatly by stripping them out so the anonymous requests all look the same.

Here is a simple example that will bypass the cache for logged-in users and strip the cookies for anonymous users[25]:

---

 https://www.varnish-cache.org/docs/4.0/users-guide/vcl-backends.html#directors ↗

 The name `sessionid` is the Django default, but can be configured using the `SESSION_COOKIE_NAME` setting.

```
sub vcl_recv {
  # bypass the cache for logged in users
  if (req.http.cookie ~ "sessionid" ){
    return (pass);
  } else {
    unset req.http.Cookie;
  }
  return (hash);
}
```

Another helpful snippet you can place in your `vcl_recv` is a cache bypass mechanism. This will check for the presence of a pre-defined URL parameter and, if defined, pass the request straight to the backend. These can be handy for troubleshooting.

```
if (req.url ~ "(\?|&)flush-the-cache") {
    return(pass);
}
```

If you use the same name you defined earlier for your template cache (see Custom Cache Template Tag *(page 44)*), it will give you a simple way to bust straight through your cache all the way down to the application and database layers.

This subroutine is also a good place to handle permanent redirects, domain name normalization, and dropping requests for URLs that you know don't exist in Django (`/favicon.ico` for example). Remember, the more requests you can stop here, the less work your application needs to do. Here's an example that drops all requests for common static files:

```
if (req.method == "GET" &&
    req.url ~ "\.(jpg|jpeg|png|gif|ico|js|css)$") {
```

```
return (synth(404, "Not Found"));
}
```

IMPROVING YOUR HIT RATE

This simple setup will get you up and running with Varnish, but you'll probably have a lot of room for improvement on your cache hit rate. The Varnish docs have some recommendations on how to improve your hit rate[26]. If your site is mostly anonymous traffic, this will get you pretty far.

On sites where users are logged in and page content varies for every user, things become more challenging. The solution you choose will be very specific to your application, but the basic technique will probably be the same. You'll need to think about how you can split up your pages such that some expensive parts *don't* vary per user. In some cases, the only difference is the user name displayed on the screen. For these sorts of pages, you can still take advantage of Varnish by splitting up the page and using a two-phase rendering process.

One option is to have Django render an anonymized version of the page for Varnish to cache, then use AJAX to make an additional request filling in the personalized bits. This gets the initial page to the user as quickly as possible, but there will be a delay as the second request is fired to get the personalized information.

The other option is to use ESI (Edge Side Includes) and let Varnish use that information to assemble the page for you. For more details on this

---

[26] https://www.varnish-cache.org/docs/4.0/users-guide/increasing-your-hitrate.html ↗

approach, see Varnish's Edge Side Includes documentation [27].

GRACE PERIODS

Grace periods are a lesser known gem inside Varnish that lets you serve stale content from cache if your application servers become unavailable.

Here is a simple VCL snippet to enable this feature:

```
vcl 4.0;
import std;

backend default {
  .host = "127.0.0.1";
  .port = "8080";
  .probe = {
    .url = "/";
    .interval = 5s;
    .timeout = 1s;
    .window = 5;
    .threshold = 3;
  }
}

sub vcl_hit {
  if (obj.ttl >= 0s) {
    # A pure unadulterated hit, deliver it
    return (deliver);
  }
  if (!std.healthy(req.backend_hint) ||
      (obj.ttl + obj.grace > 0s)) {

    # backend not healthy or within the grace window
    return (deliver);
  }
  return (fetch);
```

27   https://www.varnish-cache.org/docs/4.0/users-guide/esi.html

```
}

# Happens after reading the backend response headers
sub vcl_backend_response {
  set beresp.grace = 6h;
  # Force the TTL to 20s
  set beresp.ttl = 20s;
  return (deliver);
}
```

NOTE

Every 5 seconds, Varnish is going to probe your application server at the URL defined (in this case, "/") to determine if it is healthy. If less than 3 (`threshold`) out of 5 (`window`) probes pass, the backend is declared unhealthy. See the Varnish docs on health checks[28] for more details.

To confirm your configuration is working:

1. Fetch a URL in Varnish, loading it into the cache.

2. Wait for the content to expire (in this case the TTL is 20 seconds).

3. Drop your application server by killing the uWSGI process.

4. Fetch the same URL through Varnish again.

On the second fetch, you should see a response like this:

[28] https://www.varnish-cache.org/docs/4.0/users-guide/vcl-backends.html#health-checks⬈

```
$ curl -I http://127.0.0.1:6081/
HTTP/1.1 200 OK
Content-type: text/html
Last-Modified: Mon, 17 Feb 2014 10:19:03 GMT
Date: Mon, 17 Feb 2014 10:55:14 GMT
X-Varnish: 976346113 976346109
Age: 127
Via: 1.1 varnish-v4
Connection: Keep-Alive
```

Note the `Age: 127` header. This tells you the number of seconds since Varnish fetched this page from your web server. If it is greater than the TTL, but you still receive the cached page content, you're in business.

Congratulations, you're now serving Django without Django! Varnish's grace periods are a nice safety net when the unexpected (but inevitable) happens, and can buy you some time to get things back into working order.

CUSTOM ERROR PAGE

Error 503 Backend fetch failed

Backend fetch failed

Guru Meditation:

XID: 9

Varnish cache server

You've probably seen one of these at some point while browsing the web. It's Varnish's default error page and, as you can see, it isn't particularly user friendly. To provide a nicer HTML page to the end user when your application fails, use a snippet like this:

```
sub vcl_backend_error {
    # Otherwise, return the custom error page
    set beresp.http.Content-Type = "text/html; charset=utf-8";
    synthetic(std.fileread("/var/www/error.html"));
    return(deliver);
}
```

REDIRECTS

Since Varnish is so fast, it's a good place to handle any hard-coded redirects you might need to serve your application. Unfortunately, Varnish doesn't provide a built-in "redirect" command, so you need to jump through a couple hoops to make it happen.

Here's an example of redirecting requests on the "naked" domain to the `www.` subdomain.

```
sub vcl_recv {
  if (req.request == "GET" &&
      req.http.host == "example.com") {

    return (synth(801, "http://www.example.com" + req.url));
  }
  return (hash);
}

sub vcl_synth {
  if (resp.status == 801) {
```

```
      set resp.http.Content-Type = "text/html; charset=utf-8";
      set resp.http.Location = resp.reason;
      set resp.status = 301;
   }
   return (deliver);
}
```

The redirects can be conditional on any number of variables beyond just `url`, including paths, cookies, and headers.

The use of `801` is somewhat arbitrary. We're taking advantage of an undefined HTTP status code that we know will only come from inside Varnish. This effectively creates a GOTO statement which passes redirects to a Varnish function that can send a response to the user. Similarly, you could use status code `802` to handle temporary `302` redirects.

PURGING THE CACHE

In some situations it's handy to be able to purge a single URL from Varnish's cache immediately. This is another case where we'll stray from the HTTP specs and implement a custom method named `PURGE`.

```
sub vcl_recv {
   if (req.method == "PURGE"){
      return(purge);
   }
   return (hash);
}
```

The example above lets you craft an HTTP request that will force Varnish to invalidate its cache for the given URL.

```
$ curl -I -XPURGE http://localhost:6081/
HTTP/1.1 200 Purged
Date: Wed, 16 Jul 2014 07:56:09 GMT
Server: Varnish
X-Varnish: 9
Content-Length: 0
Connection: keep-alive
Accept-Ranges: bytes
```

!WARNING!

Be careful, this could allow a malicious hacker to execute a DDoS on your site by continuously bypassing your cache. See the Varnish documentation on purging[29] for how to use `acl` to define which IPs are allowed to issue a PURGE request.

CONFIGURING YOUR SERVERS

The prevalence of cloud servers and good configuration management tools has made it possible to get complex server farms up and running

---

[29] https://www.varnish-cache.org/docs/4.0/users-guide/purging.html#http-purging

without being a systems administration guru. This is a blessing and a curse because you can end up in the deep-end of the pool without ever having learned how to swim. Once you have your server farm deployed, you need to make sure you haven't left the doors wide open for the bad guys to waltz right in. In addition, you have to ensure your data is safe in the event of a hardware catastrophe (or fat fingers). We'll just touch on some basics of system administration here, but if you don't have anyone on your team that has experience managing servers, consider some further reading on the subject[30].

SECURITY

While most modern distributions are reasonably secure out of the box, there's a few more steps you should take for a machine that will be accessible on the public internet. Here's a bare minimum list to consider. If you are deviating from it, make sure you fully understand the risk and possible ramifications.

LOCK DOWN SSH

Disable `root` login (use `sudo`) and disable password logins (keys are stronger) with the following two lines in `/etc/sshd_config`:

```
PermitRootLogin no
PasswordAuthentication no
```

---

[30] UNIX and Linux System Administration Handbook
(http://www.amazon.com/dp/0131480057/ ⬀), Essential System Administration
(http://shop.oreilly.com/product/9780596003432.do ⬀)

You may also want to consider changing the port SSH listens on as an additional measure using the `Port` variable. While a savvy black hat can still find it, it will be hidden from the swarm of automated scripts that test SSH on port 22.

PATCH REGULARLY

Establish, and stick to, a schedule to patch your servers at least every few weeks. Have a plan in place for expediting critical zero-day patches (e.g., Heartbleed).

USE THE PRIVATE NETWORK

Most cloud server providers offer private networks that are only accessible to the servers within your account. Connecting your servers on the private network makes it harder for people to snoop on your traffic. A nice side effect is that the internal network is often a cheaper path between servers because providers rarely meter traffic on them.

PROTECT INTERNAL SERVICES

Internal services include things like dashboards, development servers, or your continuous integration system. They can also become a back-door into your protected network, leading to a breach. Lock them down with a VPN or an authentication proxy like Bitly's google_auth_proxy[31]. If you don't use a VPN, make sure critical data and login credentials are always sent over SSL/HTTPS.

---

[31]   https://github.com/bitly/google_auth_proxy ↗

Locking down your development environments will also ensure that Google doesn't accidentally crawl it, killing your SEO in the process :)

FIREWALL

Only allow traffic into your server on the ports and IPs you're expecting. Hardware firewalls are great, but even software firewalls like `iptables` will get the job done.

DON'T RUN AS ROOT

Use the principle of least privelege[32] to make it harder for someone to leverage a RCE (remote code execution) to gain root level access to your server. This applies to standard users logging onto the server as well. Use `sudo`, but only when necessary.

SECURE YOUR THIRD-PARTY ENDPOINTS

Locking down your servers won't help you at all if somebody can modify your code on GitHub, delete servers from your IaaS (infrastructure as a service), or steal your password reset confirmations via a hijacked email account. Use strong passwords and enable two-factor authentication when possible.

[32] http://en.wikipedia.org/wiki/Principle_of_least_privilege

BACKUP

Backups: you absolutely must have them. If you woke up and all your servers were gone, what would you be missing? Your configuration management system should be able to get the infrastructure up and running quickly, but you'll also need all the data in your database and anything that might have been uploaded by your users.

For your database, having a live replica of it running next to the primary database can make it easy to switch over in the event of a disaster. It also makes it easier to take full backups without interrupting your live site.

We recommend taking full database snapshots (via `pg_dump` or `mysqldump`) at least nightly. Also consider a log shipping solution like WAL-E[33] for point-in-time backups. If you're using a hosted database solution such as Amazon RDS or Heroku Postgres, this may already be taken care of for you.

In the old days, it was critical to maintain a current copy of your backups off-site in case of a catastrophe in your data center. While still important, the concept of off-site is a bit more nebulous in the cloud. Depending on the level of risk you're willing to assume, "off-site" could be:

- A storage provider such as Amazon S3

- A server in a different datacenter with the same provider

- A totally different cloud/colo provider

A few more questions you should consider with regard to backups:

[33]   https://github.com/wal-e/wal-e ↗

- If somebody hacks into one of your servers, can they delete or corrupt your backups? Pulling to the backup server might be better than push for this reason.

- How bad would it be if somebody got their hands on your backups? Consider encrypting them in such a way that a hacker couldn't decrypt them with information found on the same machine.

- Is a backup good if you haven't tested it? Schedule time to test your backups and verify they actually work.

MONITORING

❚❚ *You can't manage what you don't measure.*
BILL HEWLETT

Without monitoring, production websites are big black boxes. You have no insight into what is happening with the various pieces inside. And it is impossible to improve performance if you can't see what is happening. Moreover, a live application will behave very differently than the version running on your laptop. The different layers of the stack will often end up fighting for scarce resources (RAM, CPU, I/O), impacting the overall performance of the system. Monitoring and instrumentation are the only ways for you to gain insight into the dynamic behavior of your application infrastructure.

INSTRUMENTATION

Application instrumentation is the equivalent of the gauges on your car's dashboard. They tell you how fast you're going and what resources you're using. Your goal is to have instrumentation that can give you immediate answers to the following questions:

- What is the slowest part of my system? A time breakdown per request of Python, SQL, cache, etc. is ideal.

- What is the average response time for a request hitting Django?

- Which views are the slowest and/or consume the most time?

- Which database queries are the slowest and/or consume the most time?

- How are all these numbers changing over time?

NewRelic[34] is a fantastic tool to capture this information and can be setup very quickly. Unlike the rest of our stack, however, NewRelic is a closed-source, proprietary system. It is great to get you started, but can be expensive and lacks the flexibility of open source alternatives.

The de-facto open source metrics collection platform today is Graphite[35]. It does two things very well:

[34] http://newrelic.com/ ↗
[35] https://graphite.readthedocs.org/ ↗

1. Stores incoming numerical data in an RRD-style database.

2. Provides an API to query the data, returning either PNG graphs or JSON data.

Setting up Graphite could probably be an entire book on its own, but there are plenty of tutorials online you can follow. It's built in Django, so the setup should feel familiar. A couple of tips: check out the graphite-api project[36] for a pared down modern implementation of Graphite's API endpoint, and pair it with Grafana[37], an excellent "single-page app" dashboard for building and viewing graphs.

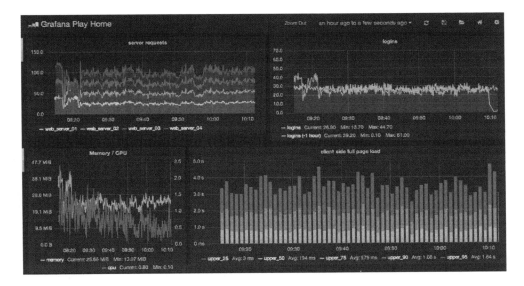

Our focus in this book is helping you collect the data you need and getting it to Graphite. In addition to instrumenting Django, you'll want to track data from all our other pieces: load balancers, web accelerators, server

[36] https://github.com/brutasse/graphite-api ↗

[37] http://grafana.org/ ↗

resources, etc. The more data you have, the easier it will be to make informed decisions about where to optimize.

Unfortunately, Django isn't built with all the hooks you need to carry out this sort of instrumentation. Thankfully, there's a package that bundles up what amounts to a series of patches to put timers in the nooks and crannies we want to instrument. Django Statsd[38], found on PyPI (Python Package Index) as `django-statsd-mozilla` due to a naming conflict, is a drop-in package which will publish the numbers we're interested in to Statsd[39]. Statsd in turn, can publish to Graphite. Alternatively, Heka can masquerade as a Statsd endpoint[40], making our stack one service simpler.

In addition to pushing to Statsd, Django Statsd can also push the data to a log or even Django Debug Toolbar, making it handy to use in local development as well.

NOTE

The current PyPI release of Django Statsd does not include the total time spent in SQL or cache for each request. This makes it difficult to graph the amount of time spent in each service per-request, similar to what NewRelic provides. Based on some similar code written by Simon Willison, we have a pull request upstream to provide this capability[41].

---

[38]   http://django-statsd.readthedocs.org/ ↗

[39]   https://github.com/etsy/statsd/ ↗

[40]   http://hekad.readthedocs.org/en/latest/man/plugin.html#statsdinput ↗

[41]   https://github.com/andymckay/django-statsd/pull/59 ↗

SERVER RESOURCES

Application metrics are important, but they don't make a difference if your server runs out of disk space or starts swapping. Be sure you push your servers vital signs into your preferred monitoring tool including:

- Load average

- CPU load

- Physical memory usage

- Disk utilization

- Network I/O

Again, NewRelic can handle this or you can push to Graphite using any number of tools. Collectd[42] is also a popular option, or for a pure Python service, consider the Diamond project[43] by Brightcove. At Lincoln Loop, we use Salt to collect and push this information to Graphite. Since we already use it, it's one less process we have to manage.

ALERTING

The next logical step in monitoring is to receive alerts when a metric starts getting into the warning zone. It's much easier to deal with problems before they become catastrophic, affecting the business and your end-users. Alerting may seem easy on the surface, but it's a tough problem to get right and a place where mistakes can hurt badly.

---

[42] https://collectd.org/ ↗
[43] https://github.com/BrightcoveOS/Diamond ↗

NewRelic has basic alerting baked in. "Serious" open source tools like Nagios[44] and Riemann[45] can interact with Graphite, but also come with a steep learning curve. Less mature options such as Django-based Cabot[46], seyren[47], and rearview[48] are also available.

A few ideas on when to send alerts:

- Errors are above X% of requests

- Server down

- High server utilization: load, swap, disk, etc.

- Service not responding

LOGGING

Not all data can easily be boiled down to a single number for Graphite. For everything else, you'll want to use a log aggregator. Splunk[49] and Loggly[50] are popular commercial services, but we prefer the combination of ElasticSearch[51], Kibana[52], and Heka[53] which provides similar

---

[44] http://www.nagios.org/ ↗

[45] http://riemann.io/ ↗

[46] http://cabotapp.com/ ↗

[47] https://github.com/scobal/seyren ↗

[48] https://github.com/livingsocial/rearview/ ↗

[49] http://www.splunk.com/ ↗

[50] https://www.loggly.com/ ↗

[51] http://www.elasticsearch.org/ ↗

[52] http://www.elasticsearch.org/overview/kibana/ ↗

[53] http://hekad.readthedocs.org/ ↗

functionality in an open source package. You may also see people using Logstash[54] in place of Heka to accomplish the same task.

This layout is very similar to the stack we prescribed with Graphite.

- Kibana :: Grafana (dashboard)

- ElasticSearch :: Graphite (storage/API)

- Heka :: Statsd (transport)

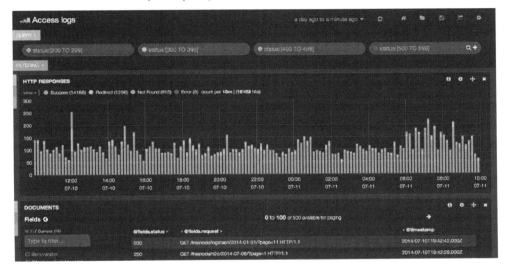

Once your app is spread across several systems, grepping log files can be very challenging and finding patterns is almost impossible. Kibana presents all that text data in a visual fashion. You can use it to search for specific log conditions, present histograms of those events over time, break down or segment the info, and much more. When you hit a tougher problem that requires searching for the needle in the haystack, or you need data to back-up an ops-related theory, this combo is invaluable.

54   http://logstash.net/

You'll want to collect:

- Apache-style logs that go all the way from your Load Balancer down to your application, ideally with a unique stamp that will let you track the request as it traverses your stack.

- Any in-application logging.

- Syslogs of any critical services.

- At a minimum, slow database queries but possibly all queries if you can ship them without causing I/O contention with the database (separate disk or over the network).

ERROR REPORTING

Django's default method of error reporting is to email a site administrator when a traceback is encountered in production. This feature is a blessing on low-traffic websites where errors might otherwise go unnoticed. On high-traffic websites, however, this feature can cause serious problems.

1. Email is a horrible tool for tracking frequency in errors and changes over time.

2. If you end up with an error on a high-traffic page, you can DoS your mail server, get blacklisted, or have your email provider pull the plug on your service (they tend to frown upon 10k emails being sent in a couple seconds).

Luckily, better options for error reporting already exist. Again NewRelic is an option here, but the open source Sentry[55] project is better suited to this task. Like Graphite, it is written in Django. Originally an internal tool at Disqus, it has spun-off into its own product with both a paid hosted version and free local installation options. Sentry will give you a nice dashboard to track errors in your application. You can send error reports from a number of other languages beyond just Python with it's client application, raven[56]. There's even a JavaScript version that will let you track errors in your client-side code as well. With Sentry, instead of getting hit with 10k emails, it will only email you on the *first* one, then collect and aggregate the rest in its web interface for analysis.

TIP

On the topic of errors, one drawback to having multiple layers in front of your application is that an error could be raised at any level in the stack. Even if you have a pretty Django 500.html template setup, your web accelerator and load balancer will return ugly un-styled pages if they encounter an error trying to communicate with the next layer in the stack. As part of your deployment process, you'll want to make sure you dump out a flat HTML file and configure these services to use it.

---

[55] https://www.getsentry.com/ ↗
[56] https://github.com/getsentry?query=raven ↗

At this point, you should have your server farm operational, but how do you know it is ready for production traffic? In the next chapter we'll discuss launch preparation so you can confidently take your site into production.

THE PREPARATION

CHAPTER 4
THE PREPARATION

❚❚ *Before anything else, preparation is the key to success.*
ALEXANDER GRAHAM BELL

With your Django site deployed to live servers, you'll probably either be excited to show the world your project or terrified it will fall flat on its face when the barrage of real world traffic hits. If you're in the excited camp, you need to cool your jets, there's still more work to do. If you're terrified, let's take some steps to quell your fear.

Up to now, we've made educated guesses at where the hot spots will be in your application. But educated guesses can only take you so far. It's time to load test the system and collect real data to know if, and where, further optimization is required. Starting this process early in your development cycle will save you time by showing you exactly where optimization is needed, and when you've reached "good enough".

LOAD TESTING WITH JMETER

There are a number of tools available that let you generate a flood of HTTP traffic to see where and when your servers start to topple over. Apache Bench (ab)[1] and Siege[2] are popular and easy to use tools for basic sanity checking, but for more robust tests, Jmeter is king.

Jmeter is one of those Java apps you love to hate. It's really powerful, but comes with a steep learning curve and a nonintuitive interface. It can be configured and run via a GUI or from the command line with an XML configuration file.

We typically build out a test plan in the GUI, then export it to XML for automated headless testing. To get started, you'll want to create a `user.properties` file with the following values:

```
CookieManager.delete_null_cookies=false
CookieManager.save.cookies=true
jmeter.save.saveservice.url=true
jmeter.save.saveservice.requestHeaders=true
```

These values ensure we have what we need to successfully authenticate against a Django site and also log some additional information that may come in handy later. Jmeter will pick up these settings when started with `jmeter -p /path/to/user.properties`.

---

[1] http://httpd.apache.org/docs/2.2/programs/ab.html ↗

[2] http://www.joedog.org/siege-home/ ↗

CONFIGURATION

First, set a few user defined variables directly on the root *Test Plan* element:

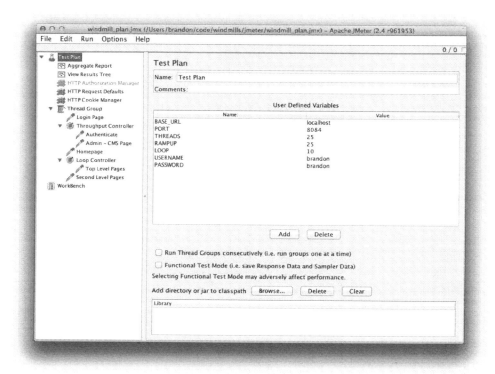

This keeps things DRY (Don't Repeat Yourself), making it easy to change the values globally rather than hunting across child elements. The THREADS setting determines how many virtual users will be accessing your site at the same time. This is similar to the concurrency option in ab.

RAMPUP allows you to slowly work your way up to the number of THREADS. By avoiding immediately hitting the same URL with a large number of simultaneous connections, your tests will be more realistic.

LOOP is the number of times each thread will loop through the test plan. For example, if you have 50 threads and a loop value of 10, your plan will be executed 500 times. It is important for your test to run long enough to spot issues with things like cache invalidation or key eviction.

These settings can be included in test plan elements using Java string substitution: `${my_variable_name}`. This tells JMeter to read a variable or execute a function.

GENERATING REQUESTS WITH SAMPLERS

First create a Thread Group by right-clicking on the *Test Plan* element, then selecting *Add → Threads (Users) → Thread Group*. Once the element is created, fill in the "Thread Properties" with your settings variables from the *Test Plan* element.

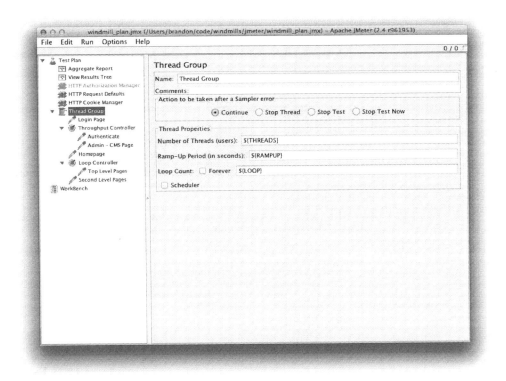

Next, right-click the thread group and select *Add → Sampler → HTTP*

Request to create a sampler element. You'll see there are lots of ways to customize your request. The most important ones to get started are "Server Name or IP" and "Path".

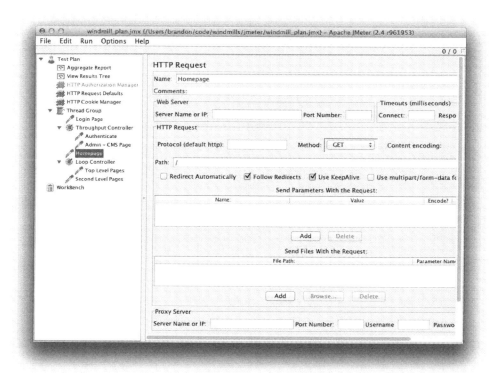

JMeter provides an easy way to manage these globally with the "HTTP Request Defaults" config element. Right-click on your *Test Plan* element, and select *Add → Config Element → HTTP Request Defaults*. There, you can enter your domain, port, and any other detail you want to apply to all "HTTP Request" samplers within the same scope.

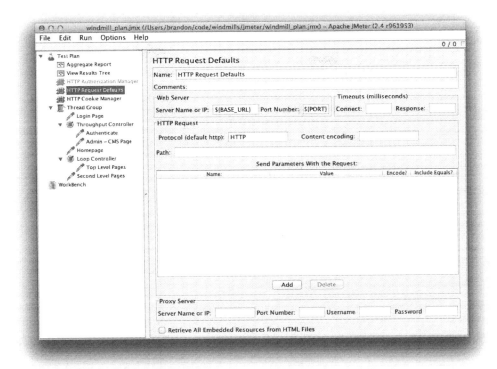

At this point, you can run the Test Plan. Use `Control-R` to start it and stop it with `Control-+`. On OS X, use `Command` instead of `Control`.

GATHERING DATA WITH LISTENERS

To collect useful data from the tests, add a Listener to your Test Plan. Two of the most useful Listeners are *Aggregate Report* and *View Results Tree*.

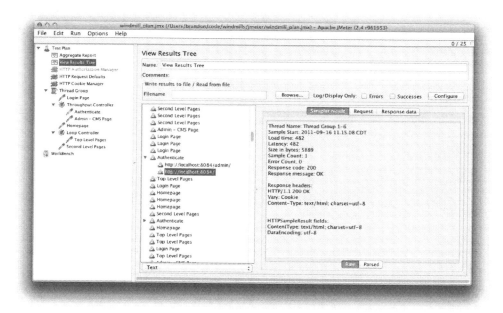

The Results Tree provides details of each request JMeter generates. It is useful for tracking down errors in your plan or application.

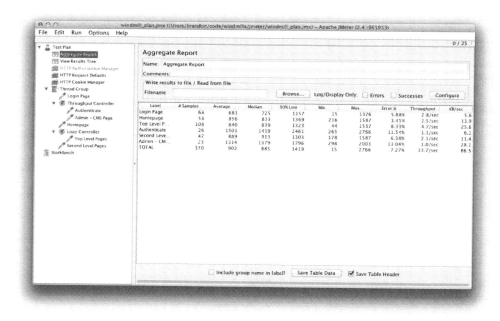

The Aggregate Report gives you rolled up statistics, separated by sampler with a total at the bottom.

RETRIEVING DATA FROM A TEXT FILE

JMeter provides access to a variety of functions within your test plans. One particularly useful function is `StringFromFile()`. It retrieves data from a text file separated by newlines. The path of the file is relative to where you launched JMeter, so we keep our data in a `data` subdirectory within the `jmeter` folder we created earlier.

HTTP Request

Name: Second Level Pages

Comments:

Web Server | Timeouts (milliseconds)
Server Name or IP: | Port Number: | Connect: | Res|

HTTP Request

Protocol (default http): | Method: GET | Content encoding:

Path: /${_StringFromFile(data/top-level.txt)}/${_StringFromFile(data/second-level.txt)}/

☐ Redirect Automatically   ☑ Follow Redirects   ☑ Use KeepAlive   ☐ Use multipart/form-data

Send Parameters With the Request:

This is great for dynamically constructing URLs. Each time JMeter encounters the `StringFromFile()` function for a particular file, it will read the next line in the file.

For example, if you had a URL in the form of `/articles/my-article-slug/`, you could keep a collection of slugs in a text file like this:

```
a-very-interesting-article
an-even-better-article
not-quite-as-good-but-still-fascinating
this-is-the-last-one-i-swear
```

Then, in the *HTTP Sampler*, refer to the path as
`/articles/${_StringFromFile(data/my-text-file.txt)}/` to
cycle through each article slug in the list.

This technique makes it easy to use an individual sampler for testing
multiple pages on your site.

TIP

*If you are replacing an existing site and have access to Apache style traffic
logs, you can feed them directly into JMeter to replay the traffic against your
new site. We have a write-up on our blog[3] with more details.*

LOGGING IN

Django's CSRF protection makes authentication with JMeter slightly more
challenging. This is where the `CookieManager.save.cookies=true`
property comes in handy. The *HTTP Cookie Manager* config element
saves cookies as variables, which can be referenced as
`${COOKIE_cookiename}`.

---

[3] http://lincolnloop.com/blog/load-testing-jmeter-part-3-replaying-apache-logs/ ↗

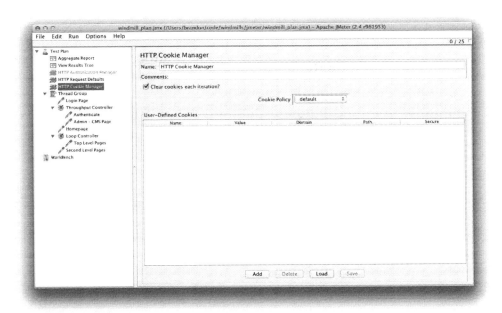

Enabling "Clear cookies each iteration" clears the cookies at the end of each loop giving each test loop a clean slate.

To handle authentication, simply create an "HTTP Request" using the POST method.

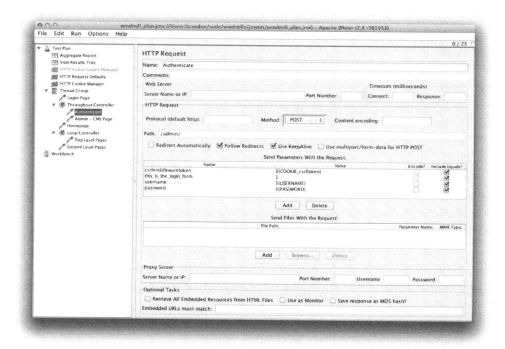

This is an example of logging in to Django's admin. Note the "Method" is POST, and the following parameters have been added:

- `csrfmiddlewaretoken`: `${COOKIE_csrftoken}`. A cookie automatically added by the CSRF Middleware on pages which require it.

- `this_is_the_login_form`: 1 Required for the Django admin login form.

- `username` Uses the global Test Plan variable.

- `password` Uses the global Test Plan variable.

Once a thread logs in, all its subsequent requests will be authenticated, until the cookies are cleared.

AJAX REQUESTS

If your application behaves differently for AJAX requests, you can fake them in JMeter by adding the `X-Requested-With: XMLHttpRequest` header.

To do this, right click on the thread group and select *Add → Logic Controller → Simple Controller*.

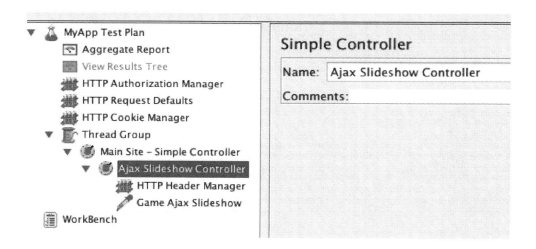

Once it's named, right-click it and select *Add → Config Element → HTTP Header Manager*. Create the "X-Requested-With" header with the value "XMLHttpRequest".

Finally, create the *HTTP Request* that will use the special header.

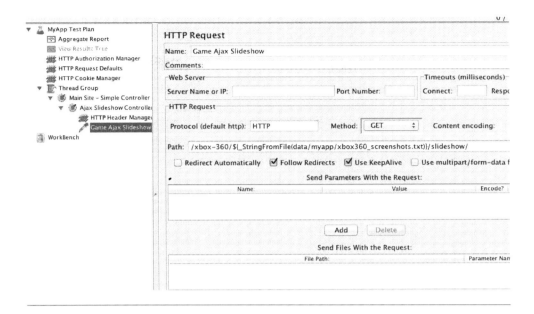

This should give you what you need to run JMeter from your local computer against your development or soon-to-be production infrastructure. Running load tests from your local machine, however, is problematic for a couple of reasons. First, you may not have enough bandwidth to really saturate your site with connections. Second, you don't want to tie up your local machine running slow load tests when you could be working.

It's better to run a headless instance of JMeter from within your own infrastructure. This will remove the network complications of running it locally. You could run it from an unused dev server within the same network or spin up a cloud server with JMeter on-demand. We recommend not running it directly on a machine you'll be testing because the additional load from JMeter will throw off the results.

JMeter can be installed with your package manager on most distributions.

For Ubuntu/Debian, `apt-get install jmeter` will get you going.

Once installed, copy the `jmeter` folder you created earlier up to the server, then fire it up with the following CLI (command line interface) incantation:

```
jmeter -n -p user.properties \
       -t my_test_plan.jmx \
       -l my_results.jtl
```

- `-n` is "nogui" mode

- `-p` is the path to the user.properties file

- `-t` is the path to the test plan

- `-l` is the path where JMeter should log the results

REVIEWING THE LOG

When the test plan is done, the easiest way to view the results is to copy the `.jtl` it created back to your local machine and open it in the JMeter GUI. From a listener, there is a *Write results to file / Read from file*. Click on the "Browse" button there, and navigate to your `.jtl` file.

Aggregate Report

Name:	Aggregate Report
Comments:	

Write results to file / Read from file

Filename		Browse...

Label	# Samples	Average	Median	90% Line	
TOTAL	0	0	0	0	922

This loads up the listener as if you had run the test locally.

INTEGRATING WITH JENKINS

Manually running JMeter, copying, and loading up the results to inspect them gets cumbersome quickly. It also makes it hard to spot regressions in performance over time. If you use Jenkins for continuous integration, then its "Performance Plugin"[4] can be used to review graphical results, illustrating performance trends over time.

Here's a simple script you can run in Jenkins:

```bash
#!/bin/bash

# Clear out old results
rm $WORKSPACE/jmeter.jtl

# Run the tests
cd "$WORKSPACE/jmeter"

jmeter -n -t test_plan.jmx \
```

---

[4] https://wiki.jenkins-ci.org/display/JENKINS/Performance+Plugin ↗

```
-l "$WORKSPACE/report.jtl" \
-p user.properties
```

In the "Post-build Actions" section, enable the "Publish Performance test result report" action. In the "Report files" field, point the plugin to your log file, `report.jtl`.

At this point you can save the configuration, and you're done! The performance test will run regularly on the schedule you entered, or you can run a test at any time using "Build Now".

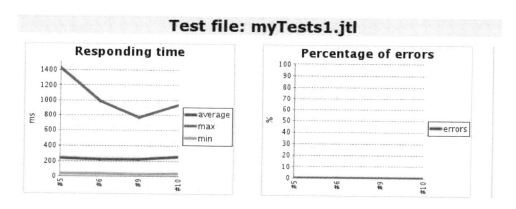

INTERPRETING THE RESULTS

Load testing with JMeter should give you a good indication of whether your site is capable of handling lots of traffic without falling flat on its face. But what if it's not? How will you know?

You should get into a feedback cycle with JMeter in which you run a test, interpret the results, make calculated optimizations, and then re-test. Of course, you want to analyze JMeter's output to make sure your error rate is zero (or very close to it) and that your response times are acceptable, but you also need to monitor your servers during the test runs. Confirm that your cache hit rates are healthy and no single service is running too hot, exhausting the server's resources. This will give you a good chance to hone the skills you'll need to effectively monitor and manage your production launch. We'll go into further detail in The Launch *(page 133)* chapter.

LAUNCH PLANNING

The common expectation for a new site/feature launch is that you flip the switch one day and it is immediately live for all your users to see. This is a risky plan for a few reasons. No matter how much testing and planning you've done, you'll never cover *every* possible scenario. And if there is a fault in the system, you are guaranteeing it will be a spectacular one affecting all your users. A better approach is to ease traffic onto the new system, allowing you to watch how it behaves and to react in a calm, calculated manner. In contrast, opening the flood gates will surely be a stressful event and have your team scrambling to patch holes on the fly.

In some cases, business needs will trump those of engineering and flipping the switch is the only viable option. In this scenario, you'll either use DNS or load balancers to point traffic to your new application servers, with your team on high alert (more on that in the next chapter).

If you're fortunate enough to be able to take a more calculated approach, there are a few different techniques to ease traffic onto your new infrastructure.

1. Use your load balancers to split traffic between old and new. Make sure you have enabled session affinity or sticky sessions so users won't bounce between new and old.

2. Do a "dark launch" where users send traffic to the new infrastructure but don't actually interact with it. This can be accomplished by having certain portions of your existing site trigger background AJAX requests to the new system.[5]

3. Invisibly proxy live traffic to the new infrastructure using something like Gor[6].

4. Use feature flags to release new features to a subset of your users. The folks at Disqus[7] and Lanyrd[8] have discussed the merits of this approach and how to successfully implement it in Django.

---

[5] More info at: http://farmdev.com/thoughts/85/dark-launching-or-dark-testing-new-software-features/ ↗

[6] http://leonsbox.com/blog/2013/06/04/improving-testing-by-using-real-traffic-from-production/ ↗

[7] http://blog.disqus.com/post/789540337/partial-deployment-with-feature-switches ↗

[8] https://www.youtube.com/watch?v=WMRjj06R6jg ↗

Whichever scenario you choose, it's important to have an emergency plan. What will you do if things go horribly wrong? In a perfect world, your launch will not prevent you from rolling back to the old system for a short period in the event of a catastrophic problem. If instead you burn the bridges behind you as you go, you could find yourself stuck on a sinking island. Having these discussions up front and thinking through the ramifications can save you from making a poor decision in the heat of the moment on launch day.

PRE-LAUNCH CHECKLIST

The site is built, you have a plan to launch it, and you are confident that it can withstand the initial traffic without the servers melting to the ground. It's time for one last sanity check so you don't get caught with your pants down on launch day. Here's a checklist to make sure you've dotted your i's and crossed your t's.

DJANGO CONFIGURATION

- `DEBUG` and `TEMPLATE_DEBUG` are set to `False`

- `SECRET_KEY` is a large random string and is, in fact, secret.

- `ALLOWED_HOSTS` lists any valid domain a visitor might use to hit your site: `['.example.com']`

- `TEMPLATE_LOADERS`: Cached template loader is enabled: `(('django.template.loaders.cached.Loader', TEMPLATE_LOADERS),)`

- `SESSION_ENGINE` is something faster than the default. See SESSION_ENGINE *(page 76)* for details.

- `CACHES`: A backend for Memcached or Redis. See CACHES *(page 74)* for details.

- `MEDIA_ROOT` and `MEDIA_URL` are accepting and displaying file uploads

- Administrator accounts are limited and have strong passwords.

DEPLOYMENT

- A basic click-through of the site works as expected (no broken images or links).

- Django logs are being written to file and/or being sent to a central aggregator.

- Monitoring/metrics platform is receiving data. Make sure you can see failures at every layer of the stack.

- Errors are being reported and triggering notifications.

- Third-party services are live and receiving data (payments, analytics, etc.)

- Outbound mail is flowing from your application servers and your Celery workers.

- Custom error (500 and 404) pages are setup at every level (load balancer, web accelerator, Django).

- Django admin is not publicly available at `/admin/`.

- SSL certificate is valid and ciphers are secure[9].

- Django-secure's `manage.py checksecure` runs clean.

INFRASTRUCTURE

- Servers and services are secured and locked down.

- A simple and stable procedure is in place to deploy new code.

- You have a plan to quickly scale services horizontally if needed.

- DNS TTL dropped to 5 minutes or less if a change is required.

Are you feeling ready? It's taken a lot of effort to get here and now it's time to turn the keys and push the big red "Launch" button. In the next chapter we'll show you how to watch for problems on the big day and handle the inevitable issues that will arise.

[9] https://www.ssllabs.com/ssltest/index.html ↗

THE
LAUNCH

CHAPTER 5
THE LAUNCH

Launching is always a stressful experience. No matter how much preparation you do upfront, production traffic is going to throw you a curve ball. During the launch you want to have a 360° view of your systems so you can identify problems early and react quickly when the unexpected happens.

YOUR WAR ROOM:
MONITORING THE LAUNCH

The metrics and instrumentation we discussed earlier will give you a high-level overview of what's happening on your servers, but during the launch, you want finer-grained, real-time statistics of what's happening within the individual pieces of your stack.

Based on the load testing you did earlier, you should know where hot spots might flare up. Setup your cockpit with specialized tools so you can watch these areas like a hawk when production traffic hits.

SERVER RESOURCES

htop is like the traditional top process viewer on steroids. It can be installed on Ubuntu systems with apt-get install htop.

Use htop to keep an eye on server-level metrics such as RAM and CPU usage. It will show you which processes are using the most resources per server. htop has a few other nifty tricks up its sleeve including the ability to:

- send signals to running processes (useful for reloading uWSGI with a SIGHUP)

- list open files for a process via lsof

- trace library and syscalls via ltrace and strace

- renice CPU intensive processes

WHAT TO WATCH

- Is the load average safe? During peak operation, it should not exceed the number of CPU cores.

- Are any processes constantly using all of a CPU core? If so, can you split the process up across more workers to take advantage of multiple cores?

- Is the server swapping (Swp)? If so, add more RAM or reduce the number of running processes.

- Are any Python processes using excessive memory (greater than 300MB RES)? If so, you may want to use a profiler to determine why.

- Are Varnish, your cache, and your database using lots of memory? That's what you want. If they aren't, double-check your configurations.

VARNISH

Varnish is unique in that it doesn't log to file by default. Instead, it comes bundled with a suite of tools that will give you all sorts of information about what it's doing in realtime. The output of each of these tools can be filtered via tags[1] and a special query language[2] which you'll see examples of below.

[1] https://www.varnish-cache.org/docs/4.0/reference/vsl.html
[2] https://www.varnish-cache.org/docs/4.0/reference/vsl-query.html

VARNISHSTAT

```
Uptime mgt:    0+01:10:09
Uptime child: 0+01:10:08

 NAME                      CURRENT        CHANGE       AVERAGE         AVG_10
MAIN.uptime                  4208          1.00          1.00           1.00
MAIN.sess_conn               8573         34.95          2.00          25.61
MAIN.client_req             61439        101.86         14.00          74.61
MAIN.cache_hit              43306         52.93         10.00          37.74
MAIN.cache_miss                54          0.00            .            0.00
MAIN.backend_conn           18198         46.94          4.00          36.84
MAIN.backend_toolate        18195         48.93          4.00          36.97
MAIN.backend_recycle        18196         47.94          4.00          36.87
MAIN.fetch_length              33          0.00            .            0.00
MAIN.fetch_eof              18160         47.94          4.00          36.87
MAIN.fetch_304                  3          0.00            .            0.00
MAIN.pools                      2          0.00            .            2.00
MAIN.threads                  200          0.00            .          200.00
MAIN.threads_created          200          0.00            .            0.00
MAIN.n_object                 111         -1.00            .          110.98
MAIN.n_objectcore             164          0.00            .          163.85
MAIN.n_objecthead              95          0.00            .           95.00
  MAIN.uptime                                                          INFO
Child process uptime:
```

You'll use `varnishstat` to see your current hit-rate and the cumulative counts as well as ratios of different events, e.g. client connections, cache misses, backend connection failures, etc.

VARNISHHIST

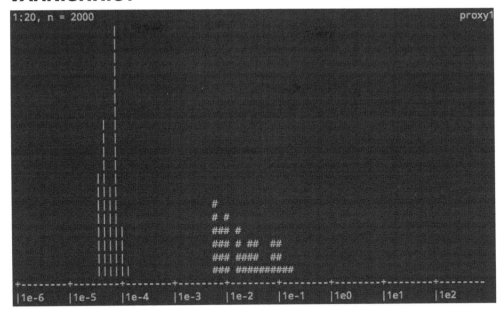

varnishhist is a neat tool that will create a histogram of response times. Cache hits are displayed as a | and misses are #. The x-axis is the time it took Varnish to process the request in logarithmic scale. 1e-3 is 1 millisecond while 1e0 is 1 second.

VARNISHTOP

```
list length 41880                                               proxy1

    571.87 VCL_call        RECV
    571.62 ReqMethod       GET
    485.77 RespProtocol    HTTP/1.1
    398.02 VCL_return      deliver
    350.62 VCL_call        DELIVER
    280.42 Debug           RES_MODE 2
    141.52 RespHeader      Vary: Cookie
     92.17 ReqHeader       Host: 104.131.222.114
     88.12 VCL_return      lookup
     53.42 BereqHeader     Host: 104.131.222.114
     50.77 VCL_return      fetch
     50.47 VCL_call        BACKEND_FETCH
     38.87 RespHeader      Via: 1.1 varnish-v4
     34.87 VCL_Log         [DEBUG] in vcl_hit
     33.42 BerespHeader    Vary: Cookie
     33.02 VCL_call        HASH
     32.52 ReqProtocol     HTTP/1.1
     24.38 RespHeader      Accept-Ranges: bytes
     23.47 RespHeader      Accept-Ranges: bytes
     19.55 RespHeader      Accept-Ranges: bytes
```

`varnishtop` is a continuously updated list of the most common log entries with counts. This isn't particularly useful until you add some filtering to the results. Here's a few incantations you might find handy:

- `varnishtop -b -i "BereqURL"` Cache misses by URL – a good place to look for improving your hit rate

- `varnishtop -c -i "ReqURL"` Cache hits by URL

- `varnishtop -i ReqMethod` Incoming request methods, e.g. GET, POST, etc.

- `varnishtop -c -i RespStatus` Response codes returned – sanity check that Varnish is not throwing errors

- `varnishtop -I "ReqHeader:User-Agent"` User agents

VARNISHLOG

`varnishlog` is similar to tailing a standard log file. On it's own, it will spew everything from Varnish's shared memory log, but you can filter it to see exactly what you're looking for. For example:

- `varnishlog -b -g request -q "BerespStatus eq 404" \`
  `-i "BerespStatus,BereqURL"`

  A stream of URLs that came back as a 404 from the backend.

WHAT TO WATCH

- Is your hit rate acceptable? "Acceptable" varies widely depending on your workload.

- Are URLs you expect to be cached actually getting served from cache?

- Are URLs that should *not* be cached, bypassing the cache?

- What are the top URLs bypassing the cache? Can you tweak your VCL so they are cached?

- Are there common 404s or permanent redirects you can catch in Varnish instead of Django?

UWSGI

uwsgitop shows statistics from your uWSGI process updated in realtime. It can be installed with `pip install uwsgitop` and connect to the stats

socket (see uWSGI Tuning *(page 70)*) of your uWSGI server via `uwsgitop`
`127.0.0.1:1717`.

It will show you, among other things:

- number of requests served

- average response time

- bytes transferred

- busy/idle status

Of course, you can also access the raw data directly to send to your
metrics server:

`uwsgi --connect-and-read 127.0.0.1:1717`

WHAT TO WATCH

- Is the average response time acceptable (less than 1 second)? If not,
  you should look into optimizing at the Django level as described in
  The Build *(page 17)*.

- Are all the workers busy all the time? If there is still CPU and RAM to
  spare (htop will tell you that), you should add workers or threads. If
  there are no free resources, add more application servers or upgrade
  the resources available to them.

CELERY

Celery provides both the `inspect` command[3] to see point-in-time snapshots of activity as well as the `events` command[4] to see a realtime stream of activity.

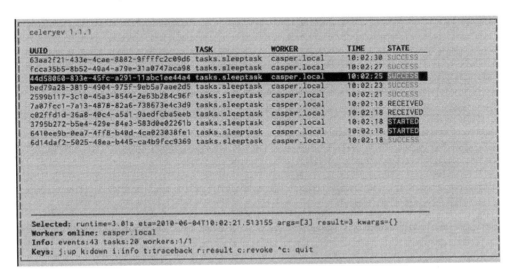

While both these tools are great in a pinch, Celery's add-on web interface, flower[5], offers more control and provides graphs to visualize what your queue is doing over time.

[3] http://celery.readthedocs.org/en/latest/userguide/monitoring.html#commands ↗

[4] http://celery.readthedocs.org/en/latest/userguide/monitoring.html#events ↗

[5] http://celery.readthedocs.org/en/latest/userguide/monitoring.html#flower-real-time-celery-web-monitor ↗

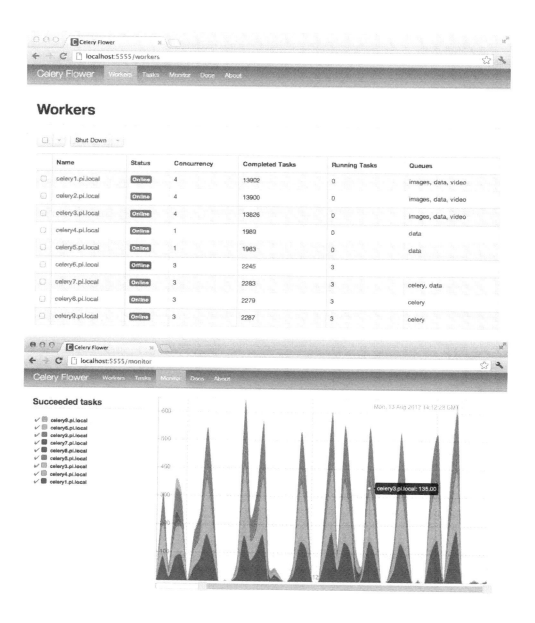

WHAT TO WATCH

- Are all tasks completing successfully?

- Is the queue growing faster than the workers can process tasks? If your server has free resources, add Celery workers; if not, add another server to process tasks.

MEMCACHED

`memcache-top`[6] will give you basic stats such as hit rate, evictions per second, and read/writes per second.

```
memcache-top v0.6          (default port: 11211, color: on, refresh: 3 seconds)

INSTANCE                    USAGE    HIT %   CONN    TIME    EVICT/s  READ/s   WRITE/s
10.209.74.65:11211          87.0%    91.7%   22      1.5ms   20.7     131.9K   319.5K
10.209.64.183:11211         89.5%    92.4%   20      0.5ms   31.3     178.6K   1.5M
10.209.104.109:11211        88.6%    93.2%   21      1.2ms   31.3     140.8K   178.8K
10.209.100.61:11211         86.7%    95.2%   19      2.0ms   26.7     251.3K   329.7K

AVERAGE:                    87.9%    93.1%   20      1.3ms   27.5     175.7K   597.9K

TOTAL:            2.1GB/    2.3GB            82      5.3ms   110.0    702.6K   2.3M
(ctrl-c to quit.)
```

It's a single Perl script that can be downloaded and run without any other dependencies:

```
curl -L http://git.io/h85t > memcache-top
chmod +x memcache-top
```

Running it without any arguments will connect to a local memcached instance, or you can pass the `instances` flag to connect to multiple remote instances:

```
./memcache-top --instances=10.0.0.1,10.0.0.2,10.0.0.3
```

[6] https://code.google.com/p/memcache-top/

WHAT TO WATCH

- How's your hit rate? It should be in the nineties. If it isn't, find out where you're missing so you can take steps to improve. It could be due to a high eviction rate or poor caching strategy for your workflow.

- Are connections and usage well balanced across the servers? If not, you'll want to investigate a more efficient hashing algorithm, or modify the function that generates the cache keys.

- Is the time spent per operation averaging less than 2ms? If not, you may be maxing out the hardware (swapping, network congestion, etc.). Adding additional servers or giving them more resources will help handle the load.

DATABASE
PG_TOP

Monitor your Postgres database activity with `pg_top`. It can be installed via `apt-get install ptop` (yes, ptop *not* pg_top) on Ubuntu. It not only shows you statistics for the current query, but also per-table (press R) and index (press X). Press E and type in the PID to explain a query in-place. The easiest way to run it is as the postgres user on the same machine as your database:

```
sudo -u postgres pg_top -d <your_database>
```

```
last pid: 29875;  load avg:  0.09,  0.07,  0.10;       up 107+03:46:44              17:03:44
15 processes: 15 sleeping
CPU states:  4.9% user,  0.0% nice,  1.7% system, 92.7% idle,  0.7% iowait
Memory: 1943M used, 52M free, 11M buffers, 1085M cached
Swap:

SEQ_SCANS SEQ_READS    I_SCANS I_FETCHES    INSERTS   UPDATES   DELETES RELNAME
173568373 22159334286          0          0      2030      7014       140 bots_channel
168328046 1566948830           0          0        70       224         0 bots_chatbot
 14139028 141255390     27984504   27984504         0     17150         0 plugins_plugin
   471316 174007279239 119948122 45148515832  76971077  54021776     67704 logs_log
   227570 4325202             28         28        28      1960        42 auth_user
    99890 2329698              0          0        98        28        28 accounts_membership
    63476 1678670              0          0         0         0         0 django_content_type
    36134 34342                0          0      1792         0      1792 social_auth_association
    28546 1372238              0          0         0         0         0 auth_permission
    22414 438172               0          0         0         0        42 social_auth_usersocialauth
    15274 15274                0          0         0         0         0 django_site
     9310 85568                0          0        84        14         0 south_migrationhistory
```

PG_STAT_STATEMENTS

If you're on a recent version of Postgres (9.2+), the `pg_stat_statements`[7] is a goldmine. On Ubuntu, it can be installed via `apt-get install postgresql-contrib`. To turn it on, add the following line to your `postgresql.conf` file:

```
shared_preload_libraries = 'pg_stat_statements'
```

Then create the extension in your database:

```
psql -c "CREATE extension pg_stat_statements;"
```

Once enabled, you can perform lookups like this to see which queries are the slowest or are consuming the most time overall.

```
SELECT
  calls
```

[7]   http://www.postgresql.org/docs/9.3/static/pgstatstatements.html

```
  round((total_time/1000/60)::numeric, 2) as total_minutes,
  round((total_time/calls)::numeric, 2) as average_ms,
  query
FROM pg_stat_statements
ORDER BY 2 DESC
LIMIT 100;
```

The best part is that it will normalize the queries, basically squashing out
the variables and making the output much more useful.

```
| calls  | total_minutes | average_ms |                                query                                |
| 102499 |          0.04 |       0.02 | SELECT "wagtailcore_site"."id", "wagtailcore_site"."hostname", "wagtailcore_site…|
|        |               |            | …"."port", "wagtailcore_site"."root_page_id", "wagtailcore_site"."is_default_site…|
|        |               |            | …" FROM "wagtailcore_site" WHERE "wagtailcore_site"."is_default_site" = ?        |
|  23692 |          0.03 |       0.09 | INSERT INTO "django_session" ("session_key", "session_data", "expire_date") VALU…|
|        |               |            | …ES (?, ?, ?)                                                                    |
| 102499 |          0.03 |       0.02 | SELECT "wagtailcore_site"."id", "wagtailcore_site"."hostname", "wagtailcore_site…|
|        |               |            | …"."port", "wagtailcore_site"."root_page_id", "wagtailcore_site"."is_default_site…|
|        |               |            | …" FROM "wagtailcore_site" WHERE "wagtailcore_site"."hostname" = ?              |
|  11846 |          0.02 |       0.10 | UPDATE "auth_user" SET "last_login" = ? WHERE "auth_user"."id" = ?              |
|  11750 |          0.02 |       0.10 |                                                                                 |
|        |               |            |                     select wp.* FROM                                            |
|        |               |            |                    wagtailcore_pagerevision wp JOIN (                            |
|        |               |            |                        SELECT max(created_at) as max_created_at, page_id FROM wagta…|
|        |               |            | …ilcore_pagerevision group by page_id                                           |
|        |               |            |                    ) as max_rev on max_rev.max_created_at = wp.created_at and wp.us…|
|        |               |            | …er_id = ? order by wp.created_at desc                                          |
|  29625 |          0.02 |       0.03 | SELECT "auth_user"."id", "auth_user"."password", "auth_user"."last_login", "auth…|
|        |               |            | …_user"."is_superuser", "auth_user"."username", "auth_user"."first_name", "auth_u…|
|        |               |            | …ser"."last_name", "auth_user"."email", "auth_user"."is_staff", "auth_user"."is_a…|
|        |               |            | …ctive", "auth_user"."date_joined" FROM "auth_user" WHERE "auth_user"."username" …|
|        |               |            | …= ?                                                                            |
```

The Postgres client's default output can be a bit hard to read. For line
wrapping and a few other niceties, start it with the following flags:

```
psql -P border=2 -P format=wrapped -P linestyle=unicode
```

For MySQL users, `pt-query-digest`[8] from the Percona Toolkit will give
you similar information.

---

[8]   http://www.percona.com/doc/percona-toolkit/2.2/pt-query-digest.html ↗

PGBADGER

While it won't give you realtime information, it's worth mentioning pgBadger[9] here. If you prefer graphical interfaces or need more detail than what `pg_stat_statements` gives you, pgBadger has your back. You can use it to build pretty HTML reports of your query logs offline.

MYTOP

The MySQL counterpart to `pg_top` is `mytop`. It can be installed with `apt-get install mytop` on Ubuntu. Use `e` and the query ID to explain it in-place.

```
MySQL on 192.168.100.172 (5.5.34-log)              up 33+10:54:28 [13:00:20]
Queries: 1.0k    qps:    0 Slow:     0.0      Se/In/Up/De(%):    1832974/00/00/00
                 qps now:   0 Slow qps: 0.0  Threads:   6 (  2/ 12) 300/00/00/00
Key Efficiency: 100.0% Bps in/out:   0.0/ 1.8  Now in/out:   8.3/ 1.8k

      Id      User       Host/IP        DB    Time   Cmd Query or State
      --      ----       -------        --    ----   --- --------------
  23299958              salt                    0   Query show full processlist
  23312579              salt                    0   Query SELECT `videos_video`.`id`, `videos_
  23312640     10.209.104.109                   0   Sleep
  23312592              salt                    1   Sleep
  23312581              salt                    5   Sleep
```

9 http://dalibo.github.io/pgbadger/

TIP

Since disks are often the bottleneck for databases, you'll also want to look at your iowait time. You can see this via `top` *as* `X%wa` *in the* `Cpu(s)` *row. This will tell you how much CPU time is spent waiting for disks. You want it to be close to zero.*

WHAT TO WATCH

- Make sure the number of connections is well under the maximum connections you've configured. If not, bump up the maximum, investigate if that many connections are actually needed, or look into a connection pooler.

- Watch out for "Idle in transaction" connections. If you do see them, they should go away quickly. If they hang around, one of the applications accessing your database might be leaking connections.

- Are queries running for more than a second? They could be waiting on a lock or require some optimization. Make sure your database isn't tied up working on these queries for too long.

- Check for query patterns that are frequently displayed. Could they be cached or optimized away?

WHEN DISASTER STRIKES

Despite all your preparation, it's very possible your systems simply won't keep up with real world traffic. Response times will sky rocket, tying up all available uWSGI workers and requests will start timing out at the load balancer or web accelerator level. If you are unlucky enough to experience this, chances are good that either your application servers, database servers, or both are bogging down under excessive load. In these cases, you want to look for the quickest fix possible. Don't rule out throwing more CPUs at the problem for a short-term band-aid. Cloud servers cost pennies per hour and can get you out of a bind while you look for longer term optimizations.

APPLICATION SERVER OVERLOAD

If the load is spiking on your application servers but the database is still humming along, the quickest remedy is to simply add more application servers to the pool (scaling horizontally). It will ease the congestion by spreading load across more CPUs. Keep in mind this will push more load down to your database, but hopefully it still has cycles to spare.

Once you have enough servers to bring load back down to a comfortable level, you'll want to use your low-level toolkit to determine why they were needed. One possibility is a low cache hit rate on your web accelerators.

NOTE

We had a launch that looked exactly like this. We flipped the switch to the new servers and watched as load quickly increased on the application layer. This was expected as the caches warmed up, but the load never turned the corner, it just kept increasing. We expected the need for three application servers, launched with four, but ended up scaling to eight to keep up with the traffic. This was well outside of our initial estimates so we knew there was a problem.

We discovered that the production web accelerators weren't functioning properly and made adjustments to fix the issue. This let us drop three application servers out of the pool, but it was still more than we expected. Next we looked at which Django views were consuming the most time. It turned out the views that calculated redirects for legacy URLs were not only very resource intensive, but, as expected, getting heavy traffic during the launch. Since these redirects never changed, we added a line in Varnish to cache the responses for one year.

With this and a few more minor optimizations, we were able to drop back down to our initially planned three servers, humming along at only 20% CPU utilization during normal operation.

DATABASE SERVER OVERLOAD

Database overload is a little more concerning because it isn't as simple to scale out horizontally. If your site is read-heavy, adding a replica (see Read-only Replicas (page 38)) can still be a relatively simple fix to buy some time for troubleshooting. In this scenario, you'll want to review the steps we took in Database Optimization (page 25) and see if there's anything you missed earlier that you can apply to your production install.

> ## NOTE
>
> *We deployed a major rewrite for a client that exhibited pathological performance on the production database at launch. None of the other environments exhibited this behavior. After a couple of dead-end leads, we reviewed the slow query log of the database server. One particular query stood out that was extremely simple, but ate up the bulk of the database's processing power. It looked something like:*
>
> ```
> ...        app_table        fk_id X
> ```
>
> *EXPLAIN told us we weren't using an index to do the lookup, so it was searching the massive table in memory. A review of the table indexes showed that the foreign key referenced in the WHERE clause was absent. The culprit was an incorrectly applied database migration that happened long before the feature actually launched, which explained why we didn't see it in the other environments. A single SQL command to manually add the index immediately dropped the database load to almost zero.*

APPLICATION & DATABASE SERVER OVERLOAD

If both your application and database are on fire, you may have more of a challenge on your hands. Adding more application servers is only going to exacerbate the situation with your database. There are two ways to attack this problem.

You can start from the bottom up and look to optimize your database. Alleviating pressure on your database will typically make your application more performant and relieve pressure there as well.

Alternatively, if you can take pressure off your application servers by tuning your web accelerator, it will trickle down to the database and save you cycles there as well.

Once you've weathered the storm of the launch, it's time to let out a big sigh of relief. The hardest work is behind you, but that doesn't mean your job is done. In the next chapter, we'll discuss maintaining your site and making sure it doesn't fall into disrepair.

THE
ROAD
AHEAD

CHAPTER 6
THE ROAD AHEAD

Once your site is launched, it's definitely time to celebrate. That's a huge accomplishment! Congratulations!

But now you need to make sure it stays up and running.

There are a few forces fighting against you in this battle:

1. Your users (via traffic spikes)

2. Your software (via bit rot)

3. You (via poor decisions)

The first one is no surprise, but after the launch, the last two are the ones that are more likely to catch you by surprise and take your site down.

TRAFFIC SPIKES

During "normal" operation, your site shouldn't be utilizing 100% of the resources at any level of the stack. Anything that regularly sits above 70% (CPU, RAM, disk, etc.) is something that should be optimized or given additional resources. While the extra resources are essentially wasted in day-to-day operation, you'll be glad you have the extra buffer when a traffic spike hits.

While some traffic spikes happen out of the blue, others are very predictable. A big marketing push or a strategic partnership, for example, might drive a major influx of traffic to your site, so make sure your business/marketing team is communicating these events to your developers. For the first few, it's a good idea to have all hands on deck just like you did on launch day. After weathering a few good bursts of traffic, you'll gain confidence with the platform and be able to predict the outcome of future events without disrupting regular development.

Withstanding your first traffic spike is the true test that you've built a system that can scale. If, however, you do run into issues, it's time to revisit Your War Room: Monitoring the Launch *(page 133)*. For sites with very "bursty" traffic patterns, you may also want to go back to A Word on Auto Scaling *(page 67)* for a cost-efficient way to handle the peaks.

BIT ROT

As you've learned, high performance sites are built on a towering stack of different services. The ability to pull mature software off-the-shelf and plug it into your infrastructure is both a blessing and a curse. On one hand, you're standing on the shoulders of giants, benefiting from years of development and testing. On the other hand, all that software needs to stay patched and up-to- date to avoid security holes or being left behind on unsupported software. Don't be surprised if from the time you started development to the time you launch at least one part of your stack is already outdated.

Part of the problem is that it's so easy to postpone this sort of housekeeping. It's usually work with no immediate benefit to your end-users or your bottom line. Teams tend to get an "if it ain't broke, don't fix it" mentality around large pieces of software, but it's a dangerous path to follow.

While it may be OK to skip a minor version here and there, you also want to make sure you don't get too far behind. If you wait too long, a few small upgrade tasks can pile up into an insurmountable mountain of work, grinding all regular development to a halt. Save your team grief by scheduling regular upgrade cycles where dependencies (your OS, major services, and Python libraries) are reviewed and updated to avoid being left behind.

POOR DECISIONS

As the developer and maintainer of a large site, you effectively are in constant contact with a loaded pistol pointed at your foot. In other words, you are your own worst enemy when it comes to keeping the site alive and healthy. It's easy to get lulled into a false sense of security once the system is finely tuned and you are deploying new code frequently. Here are a few common scenarios where you might inadvertently pull the trigger of that pistol:

ACCIDENTALLY FLUSHING THE CACHE

Restarting your cache or web accelerator during a traffic peak can be catastrophic. It's like dropping your shield and taking off your helmet in the heat of battle. All that traffic now runs straight to the slow services at the bottom of your stack. If they can't withstand the abuse while your caches warm back up, the whole site will topple over. This is commonly referred to as dog-piling or a cache stampede[1].

Thankfully, Varnish has a reload operation (`service varnish reload` on Ubuntu) so you can load a new configuration without losing the in-memory cache. Make sure your deployment tool uses this operation when you deploy configuration changes instead of opting for a hard restart.

For your other caches (memcached/Redis), you can set it up to allow you to clear portions of your cache without a full-fledged cache flush. The simplest way to do this is to have multiple entries in your `CACHES` dictionary for the different types of cache (templates, database, sessions, etc.). You use the same server instances for every one, but adjust the `KEY_PREFIX`[2] to logically separate them. Now you can invalidate an individual cache (all your templates fragments for example), by incrementing the `VERSION`[3] for that cache.

These techniques should make the need for a restart a very rare event. If a restart is absolutely necessary, during a software upgrade for example, plan it during a historically low-traffic time frame. Slowly rolling the restarts

---

[1] http://en.wikipedia.org/wiki/Cache_stampede

[2] https://docs.djangoproject.com/en/dev/ref/settings/#key-prefix

[3] https://docs.djangoproject.com/en/dev/ref/settings/#version

across each server will help too, ensuring there is only one cold cache at any given time.

LOCKING THE DATABASE

Database locks are a necessary evil but as your database gets bigger and your site gets more traffic, locks will start taking longer to release and the ramifications (temporarily blocking writes) become more problematic. Two common culprits for long database locks are schema migrations and backups.

During development, South and the built-in migrations in Django 1.7+ make changing your database schema a trivial task. Adding and removing columns only requires a couple of simple commands and might take less than a second on your development machine.

In production, however, you need to be very wary of migrations. A migration on a table with millions of rows could hold a lock for minutes while it adjusts the internal schema. This is bad news if you have users trying to write to that table at the same time.

One of the drawbacks of MySQL is that even a simple `ADD COLUMN` operation requires a full data copy of the table, completely locking it in the process. Version 5.6 has improved some operations, but this is one of the areas where PostgreSQL beats it hands-down. If you're stuck on MySQL and running into this issue, read *Taking the Pain Out of MySQL Schema Changes*[4] by Basecamp, or do what Lanyrd did and make the switch to

[4] http://signalvnoise.com/posts/3174-taking-the-pain-out-of-mysql-schema-changes ↗

PostgreSQL[5].

No matter what database you're on, migrations should always be reviewed and tested on a recent replica of your live data prior to going to production.

Backups are another cause of long database locks. Performing a dump on a sufficiently large database is going to be a time consuming process. It's best to take snapshots from a read-only replica of your live database to mitigate this issue.

MASS CACHE INVALIDATION

While not as bad as flushing the cache altogether, changing the prefix of an important set of cache keys or mass editing objects in the database will trigger a large number of cache misses and can create an influx of queries to the database. Knowing where your most frequently used or "hot" code paths are, and taking extra care with that code, will help you avoid this issue. If you're unsure about a specific change, do your deploy during a low traffic period to avoid taking your site down.

EXPENSIVE ADMIN VIEWS

It's easy to put all your focus on the user-facing side of the site and forget about your administration interface. Building an unoptimized admin view that makes a few thousand database queries isn't hard to do. But if you have a team of admins hammering on that view when your database is already hot, it can be the straw that breaks the camel's back.

---

[5]   http://www.aeracode.org/2012/11/13/one-change-not-enough/ ↗

If you are using a query cache such as johnny-cache, each save in the admin will invalidate all the cached queries for the given table. A flurry of admin activity can trigger mass cache invalidation that will put heavy pressure back on the database as the cache warms up again.

If you find yourself in a situation where admin activity is causing problems, treat it like you would any other Django view as discussed in Where to Optimize *(page 25)*.

EXPENSIVE BACKGROUND TASKS

We already discussed pushing slow tasks to background workers or performing them periodically via a cron job. But just because they operate outside of the request/response cycle doesn't mean you don't have to worry about them. Poorly optimized, database-intensive tasks can cause unexpected but regular spikes in load. In the worst case, they exceed their scheduled time window and begin to stack on top of each other. Apply the same database optimization techniques we used on your views (Database Optimization *(page 25)*) to your background tasks and keep an eye on their performance just like the rest of your stack.

GRADUAL DEGRADATION

Gradual performance degradation is a silent but swift assassin. Without keeping an eye on your metrics and being diligent about your site's performance characteristics as you add new features, you can chip away at a once well-tuned site until it topples over.

Part of your regular release process should be to watch your performance metrics (discussed in Instrumentation *(page 96)*) and look for regressions. If you see your response times or load creeping up, it's much easier to handle it immediately than try to sift through months of commits to figure out where the problem stems from.

COMPLEXITY CREEP

If you've followed along so far, you're doing a good job of keeping unnecessary complexity out of your software. You've deferred many "hard" programming problems to your database, caches, and web accelerators. As your site grows and you encounter new scaling problems, it's easy to get in the mindset that your site is a unique flower and requires equally unique solutions to keep it alive. It's fun to build your own tools, but that "not invented here"[6] attitude is dangerous in the long run. You're better off learning how to leverage Varnish more effectively now than to scrap it in favor of your own tool. The ramifications of that decision are vast:

- Training new developers is more costly. You can find a developer with experience using a service like Varnish, but your custom solution will require training every developer that walks in the door.

- Developing low-level infrastructure tools pulls development time away from your core product. With a well-supported set of source services, you effectively have a whole team of developers improving your infrastructure for free.

[6]   http://en.wikipedia.org/wiki/Not_invented_here

- Writing your own software is not a one-time cost. All software requires ongoing development, testing, documentation, etc.

While not as glamorous as the initial build-out, the process of maintaining software, keeping technical debt in check, and maximizing uptime is even more important. It's a task that favors discipline and patience so take it as an opportunity to settle in and get your Zen on.

CHAPTER 7
FINAL THOUGHTS

Now is a good time to revisit that old "Django doesn't scale" myth. What do you think? If you remember in the introduction we said it is either completely true or patently false depending on your perspective.

It's true that firing up a site with `manage.py runserver` and SQLite on a small cloud server isn't going to get you very far.

On the other hand, you've now seen the server stack we've used to build sites that handle millions of page views per day without breaking a sweat. It's the same (or very similar) to the biggest Django sites online today. In fact, you now know more about building and deploying scalable, high performance Django sites than the founding members of Instagram when they started. Back in 2012 when they were a team of three supporting the Django infrastructure for *14+ million* users, they had this to say on their engineering blog:

> *Our core principles when choosing a system are:*
>
> - *Keep it very simple*
> - *Don't re-invent the wheel*
> - *Go with proven and solid technologies when you can*[1]

We couldn't agree more. So as you continue on your Django journey, don't forget what got you here. Simplicity is the guiding philosophy.

---

[1] http://instagram-engineering.tumblr.com/post/13649370142/what-powers-instagram-hundreds-of-instances-dozens-of ↗

INDEX

ABOUT THE AUTHORS

PETER BAUMGARTNER

Peter is the founder of Lincoln Loop. While mostly involved with the business side of Lincoln Loop these days, he still enjoys learning new technology and tinkering with servers and code.

Peter is a regular conference speaker, having presented at DjangoCon and PyCon among others. His writing frequently appears on Lincoln Loop's blog and he has contributed articles to Forbes and Fast Company in the past. More recently Peter was interviewed by Basecamp and Wired about Lincoln Loop's unique style of remote work.

After a three year stint in Mexico, Peter is back in Colorado with his wife and two children and in his free time enjoys mountain biking, telemark skiing, and surfing.

YANN MALET

Also known as yml, you can usually find Yann hanging on django's IRC channels. He contributes to a number of open source apps in the Django ecosystem. Yann is passionate about building well architectured performant software.

Prior to his involvement in the Django community, Yann focused on Product Lifecycle Management systems (PLM) for several large industries as a PLM consultant for Dassault Systémes. These days, Yann enjoys a more agile career free from red tape, delivering creative and efficient software in a lean development environment.

Currently residing in Taussat, Yann enjoys surfing, running and traveling the world.

Made in the USA
Middletown, DE
18 May 2016